DATE			

Starmont Popular Culture Studies #3
(ISSN 0890-6270)

the Western Pulp Hero

An Investigation into the Psyche
of an American Legend
Written and Compiled by
Nick Carr

Starmont House, Inc.
1989

THE WESTERN PULP HERO

Library of Congress Cataloging-in-Publication Data

Carr, Wooda Nicholas.
   The western pulp hero : an investigation into the psyche of an American legend /
written and compiled by Wooda Nicholas Carr.
      p. cm. — (Starmont popular culture studies ; #3)
   Includes index.
   ISBN 1-557-42033-5 : $21.95. ISBN 1-557-42032-7 (pbk.) : $11.95
   1. Western stories—History and criticism. 2. American fiction—20th century—History and criticism. 3. Heroes in literature. 4. West (U.S.) in literature. I. Title. II.
Series: Starmont popular culture studies ; v. 3.
PS374.W4C37 1988
813'.0874'09—dc19   87-18370
                                                                      CIP

78702171

the Western PulpHero

DEDICATED
TO
RYERSON JOHNSON
and
HASCAL GILES
and
ALL OF THOSE GREAT
PULP AUTHORS
and
ARTISTS OF EARLIER DAYS

The West came alive so vividly
in their words and in their art.

CONTENTS

Doc Brimstone

Gracia

Magpie
Meyers

ACKNOWLEDGMENT

In the overall preparation of this book, my thanks must go the following individuals:

FRED COOK, who gave me my very first chance at writing about the pulps and their characters in *Bronze Shadows* magazine. This was one of the finest pulp-oriented publications of a few years ago. Issues are now in the hands of collectors.

RUTH BELCHER (God rest her soul), whose faith and devotion to the western pulp characters went beyond comprehension. She loved each one and therefore was my silent partner in this undertaking. In one sense, then, this book is also her epitaph. She now rides her golden stallion on that range beyond the stars.

LESTER BELCHER and FRED J. SIEHL, because it was from their vast collections that came many of the magazines needed. Their insight, patience and understanding served a great purpose.

To TED DIKTY, of Starmont House, who decided to take a chance and publish this book. He has the patience of a saint, and no problem was beyond him.

To the following for their encouragement when things got a little rough around the edges:
Albert Tonik, Link Hullar, Frank Lewandowski, John Gunnison, Tom and Virginia Johnson, Robert Weinberg, G. C. Burns, Franklyn Hamilton, Gary Thompson—and probably a dozen more.

RICHARD MYERS, who offered me that rare privilege of invading his pulp sanctum and collection of magazines. He is a walking encyclopedia of pulp information.

JACK and HELEN DEVENY, who always seem to make my walk along the gunsmoke trail just a little easier. No rare issue was beyond their reach.

JOHN A. DINAN, author of *The Pulp Western*, who said, "If you have need for some help here, I'd be happy to search my stuff."

DON HUTCHISON, who also opened his pulp files and offered me any assistance needed. His vast storehouse of knowledge has proven invaluable over the years I have known him. He is one of the true authorities on the bloody pulps.

HARRY (Henry) STEEGER, former President of Popular Publications in New York City, who opened many doors for me which otherwise would have remained closed.

SANDY STODDARD, of Honeyville, Utah, who reproduced the sketch of Len Siringo. Her ability with a pen is extraordinary. But then, Sandy is a remarkable lady.

ACKNOWLEDGMENT

To the following pulp authors who took pen in hand and wrote me to share their vast knowledge of the western pulps:

DAN CUSHMAN
He was the man behind the adventures of The Pecos Kid.

J. EDWARD LEITHEAD
A household name in many western pulp magazines over the years.

RYERSON JOHNSON
Friend and visitor to my hacienda in Arizona, who willingly told of his long association with the pulps.

HASCAL GILES
His name was seen in such magazines as *Masked Rider, Range Riders, Texas Rangers, West, 10 Story Western, Ranch Romances,* and many more. He told me in part: "I guess most of us who were writing stories for the western magazines in the 40s and 50s sometimes wondered who was reading them. I'm just now finding out who some of those people were."

To three of the finest western artists who ever picked up a brush. Among them they painted many of the top magazine covers during the pulp's glory era. It has been my pleasure to have met and talked with each of them:

WALTER M. BAUMHOFER

ROBERT G. HARRIS

NORMAN SAUNDERS

144 PAGES FOR 10 CENTS

STREET AND SMITH'S

WESTERN STORY MAGAZINE

AUG. 7 1937

A Complete Novel
HOT LEAD
FOR
GLEAMING
RAILS
By VON CORT

PREFACE by RYERSON JOHNSON

In the heyday of the pulps, magazines on crowded news-stands bloomed like tulips. That's from across the street where their colors flashed. Seen close-up, "outrageous" was the mildest word you could use to describe those covers. They screamed for attention with incredible action pictures, clashing colors. Within those covers high adventure waited—escape from anything that might be crowding you. Let's dab a rope on the first sentence from one of those old western stories, and see where it shakes down when the dust settles.

Here's the sentence: Up from Texas with a thousand miles of trail dust in his throat, Strap Jordan...

We don't even need to finish out that line. With a name like that, you know right off he's the good guy—barbwire tough, but good. And with a long ride like that, chewing dust all the way, you know that Strap and his trail crew are set for hooraw action. Action inside the batwing doors of the first saloon they home in on—to do something about that thousand-mile throat drought. Or maybe at the railroad stockyards in a fast and righteous explosion in fist and/or sixgun confrontation with the bad guys trying to cheat them out of their honest trail money.

9

Who wrote it?

I don't know. It could have been my story. But I wrote so many so fast, and there was such an absence of self and reality in most of those old westerns that I can read one of mine now without any sense of identification. None. My name's there at the top of it. I must have written it. But there's nothing about it to let me know. I read from line to line wondering what's going to happen next, appalled at how bad it all is. In what magazine did it appear? I don't know that either. I just somehow happened to remember that opening line. It's got western savvy and plot ingenuity.

Here's one I do remember specifically, probably because I had such a hard time selling it. *Short Stories Magazine*—November 10, 1931 issue. Ryerson Johnson—"The Mushroom Spread."

Opening line: When cow critters chew off a chunk of cholla cactus, they get a mouthful to masticate. Likewise, when Blazing Daylight Jones and Me-too Hartley attempt to. . . .

What "mouthful" are Blazing and Me-too about to try to masticate? A "spread," as western readers know, is a ranch. A mushroom ranch? You get set for that rare breed of western, a funny one.

To sell humor to a western story magazine was even harder than to sell a story where a significant role was played by a woman. In the man-action magazines, life in the West was grim and brutally earnest. Quick death stalked the cowboy's spurred heels dripping dust in the street in front of the Red Dog Saloon, or hard-riding the range in pursuit of outlaws, or just getting away from them. Humor was a jarring note. You brought in fun and levity at your peril—the peril of rejection by magazine editors dedicated to perpetuating a never-never land that existed only in the glowing imagination of the writer and in the transient "suspension of disbelief" of the reader.

Here's one more first-liner: *Star Western*—May 1940—Ryerson Johnson. The two boxcars on the siding at Flatlands loomed like huge ill-omened buzzards waiting to pick the bones of a dying town.

You didn't always open with your story people. Sometimes you varied things with the mood or circumstance. But even then you tried to get in the reader-hook. What's in those boxcars to make them seem like buzzards?

You don't wait long to develop the situation. The next line goes suchwise: Toward evening the lengthening shadows of the boxcars reached all the way to the hitchrack in front of the High Grass Saloon. The shadows mothered the brood of boxcar buzzards—tight-lipped, bleak-eyed, low-holstered hombres who lounged near the track from morning to night, following the boxcar shade around.

So now we're set with the overall menace. Time for the bad guy to show himself, and time for the good guy to come riding. . .and action or the threat of action. . .and suspensive revealment of what this boxcar stuff is all about.

There was a cliché among pulp writers that if you wanted to establish a good guy, you showed him petting a dog. A bad guy? He kicks the dog. In a western stories you could do it with a horse. Pat him or cruelly spur him. And then you're off, hard riding, on your yarn. Bad guy clobbers good guy all over the place. . .until the wind-up fight when good guy—in surprising manner—settles the score always and forever.

We didn't do much probing into personality or motivation. We generally used "character tags" to establish our characters. A line or two, sometimes a word or two, was enough to "tag' the minor characters. A few lines or a paragraph would usually suffice for the major ones. Whatever the "character tag" you decided upon, you'd return to it at intervals throughout the story to keep the reader reminded. Redhead, lantern-jawed, gentle giant, dead eyes, scar-faced, etc.—quick identification devices to keep a fast-reading reader from getting his characters mixed up.

The names generally reflected the nature of the characters. Venerable English names predominated for the heroes, particularly in western stories. Western town and county names often supplied good family names. The bad guys? Well, Scag Kelsy has *got* to be bad. Likewise, Rance Scarvy, Hack Gore, Notches Empp, Topaz Bane, Ed Spaveen, Lobo Widin. . . . Once I dreamed up a name I was sure nobody in real life would have: Wid Neff. I applied it to a particularly nefarious character. Wouldn't you know—somebody named Wid Neff in New York City called me up, purporting to be greatly perturbed and transmitting a veiled threat of lawsuit for defamation of character. I went around to meet him. He turned out to be an actors' agent, and in the conversational interchange we developed enough rapport to go down and buy each other a drink.

Sometimes I used names of childhood friends for story characters. This, I found, usually pleased, or at least amused, my friends. They didn't care what kind of character I made them—just so I worked them into the story somewhere.

Some writers were timorously careful to avoid using a real name for any unsympathetic character. Dave Dresser (Brett Halliday), at the other extreme, had fun putting nearly half the membership of the Mystery Writers of America into one of his Mike Shayne mystery novels, *She Woke to Darkness*. He killed his victims in my 510 East 38th Street apartment in New York.

Hudson River Cowboy

Maybe it's time—if you haven't already guessed it—to make my shameful admission. I was the kind of western pulp writer they called a Hudson River cowboy. Hunkered over a typewriter in a rented room in New York City, I wrote a hundred western stories before I ever went west.

I crossed the Hudson and chugged into the sunset in an old Ford Model-A convertible. I covered Colorado, Kansas, Oklahoma, Texas, Arizona and New Mexico. And later the middle and northern states. I wanted to see if the West was anything like I'd been saying.

It wasn't!

Disillusionment was complete.

Zane Grey's purple sage was a vast patch of alkali-rooted weeds, and the romantic rangeland stretched out and out under a skim-milk sky in harsh, arid, dusty, rock-and-rattlesnake cluttered miles. And the western cowboy? No more than a dry-dirt farmer with the bib cut off the top of his overalls. (That's not my original line, so someone else must be in agreement with me!)

The western writers who lived out there I'm sure had different thoughts about it. Max Band, W.C. Tuttle, S. Omar Barker, Ernest Haycox and a whole herd of others must have values that I missed in my quick once-over.

Back in New York after my western ramble, I had a problem. It was like the first time I set foot in Europe. I had known all the time it was there. But now that I was standing on it, I really knew.

Same with the stories. Now that I knew for sure I was perpetuating a western myth, it was a little harder for a while to fire myself into it. Fantasies of fist-knuckling, rope-looping, gun-blazing heroics! But you believe in the world you're creating. While you're writing you do. You have to if you're going to make the reader believe it.

I've sometimes speculated about the effect of this western myth we bloomed to life in our stories—sitting in New York and creating those adult westerns, those western fairy stories. I discovered when I went west that cowboys in their bunkhouses had stacks of western story magazines leaning against the walls. Did our characterizations affect them? Did they try to live up to that grass-roots nobility and heroism we projected? Wouldn't it be interesting if, because of the image we projected, they moved over a little in that direction?

When later I tried my luck in Hollywood (I wrangled one lone credit, a segment of *Death Valley Days* titled "Dangerous Crossing"), I discovered that there, too, western pulps were stacked against the walls. But for a different reason. Hollywood writers drew from our stories in working up situations, characters, backgrounds and premises for their scripts.

The same with us in New York. When we got stuck for a new story plot, we could go to a western movie. Somewhere along in the storyline there was bound to be a decision scene. The hero could choose to take this course of action or that one. Whichever way he went, we could go home, start with a similar opening situation and angle our story the "other way." We came out with a fresh, new story. I guess we kind of swallowed up each other, New York and Hollywood.

One time I went up to the New York Paramount office with a tear-sheet of a slick magazine story I'd sold. I hoped they'd read it as a possibiliity for a movie vehicle.

Somebody told me, "Wait a minute."

She opened a file cabinet and flipped—to Ryerson Johnson. The Paramount office had synopsized this story and every other slick-paper story I ever sold. And they'd done the same with every other slick-paper writer. But they didn't bother with pulps. Their mistake, I think. The ingenuity, the clarity of the action pattern in many of those pulps would have translated very effectively to the big screen. Well—look at TV today. Any pulp writer could merge very comfortably into the medium.

You didn't have to be in New York to sell to pulps, but it helped a little. Editors didn't like to write letters. They were phone-functional. If you were at the end of a local phone, they might get in touch with you about replacing a story they were pulling, or to "fix" a story they would have ordinarily sent back. All kinds of reasons. How about this one?

Where do you get your plots? From a cover picture and an editor's sore needs. One day Frank Gardner at *Western Aces* phoned frantically. Gardner's the one I had this interchange with the first time I went up to his office:

Q: What kind of stories do you like?

A: (Soberly, eyes squinting, lips pursed, thumb and fingers raised and squeezing together) A little bit sad.

Pretty sensitive for a pulp editor: "A little bit sad."

I could sense his meaning. Within the framework of a conventional story, an action story—a touch of emotional content somewhere to relate the yarn to the larger scene of human aspiration, longing, frustration, triumph. He was being hopeful, of course; it was hard to find writers at a-cent-a-word who would take the trouble.

On this day of the phone call he got right down to busines. "Look. We've got your name on a novelette title on the cover of the issue coming up. I don't know how it happened. Someone goofed. We've got a 24-hour printer's deadline. Can you do us 10,000 words—no more no less—to fit the space requirement? No padding. We haven't got time to cut. Use the title on the cover picture for your jump-off into the story. The picture's supposed to reflect a story scene." (The story, if I remember right, was "Comrades of the Colt.")

I'm not a fast writer. On this deal with *Western Aces* I had to be. I guess it's true that you can do what you have to do. I normally took two or three days just to muddle out a plot. Sometimes longer. But on this occasion I sat up most of the night and wrote the story. I had a wonderfully relaxed feeling about it. No uncertainty here. This one they had to take.

I have always been interested to learn how a writer chose his/her field of expression. Taking off from my own experience, I sold my first few stories to *Adventure* magazine. They were coal mine and freight-train bumming stories—two areas I knew well. Then I met a pulp-writer-turned slick—William Bryon Mowry—who told me that if I wanted to make a living writing fiction, I'd never do it with coal mines and freight trains.

"Pick up a subject people are naturally interested in," he said. I chose the Canadian Mounted Police. There were a dozen or so magazines at the time—the late 20s—running mounted police stories. With Bill's expert help I got going. But then the bottom dropped out of the mounted police world. What to do? The largest group of pulps on the news-stands were westerns. There must have been 50 titles. I decided to write westerns. I was in Urbana, Illinois at the time. I knew no more about the West than I had known about the Canadian North. I thought that all I'd have to do was read a bunch of western pulps—and I was right. I started in, reading first to get the story, reading a second time to "get the feel" of the presentation, the formula, the pacing, and to soak up some of the jargon and fictional conversations. For instance: they rarely called a revolver a revolver.

It was a six-gun, six-shooter, a .45 Colt, shooting iron, smoke pole. You could invent a likely name of your own if you wanted to. A cowboy was a cowboy sometimes, but he was also a ranny, puncher, waddy, cowpoke, ranch-hand. A ranch was almost always a "spread." The Box-K spread, the Bar X. . . . Such colorful little aberrations of the language took a while to absorb. But it's something you have to confront in working with any new background.

I started getting on with my first western story after about a week of intensive reading of western pulps, and of taking notes. I didn't sell my first one, but I sold all the rest, right up to the last one. The first one wasn't quite enough in the groove. The last one—hundreds of western stories later—was bucking an almost vanished market.

After I got into the western field I did some unified background reading—and settled on two books. I found that I could get nearly all the background information I needed from Rollins' *The Cowboy* and Webb's *The Great Plains*.

Webb supplied the historical perspective—the progression from open-range ranching to the barbwire fencing era. Plus all you needed to know about trends in the West, geography, climate, sociological interpretations—the broad sweep.

Rollins, on the other hand, was meticulous in recording the day-by-day details of cowboy life, everything from what he ate for breakfast to what he rode and wore—and his preferred branding and shooting irons. Those two books supplied all the information I needed to write hundreds of western stories.

My first western sale was to trusty old *Ace High*—a gun-trail short: "The Yucca Kid." Following along were *Western Story Weekly, Top Notch, Short Stories, Wild West, Argosy, West,* and—in the course of time—many, many others. The West of the pulp magazines was a very limited world. You could choose to write gun-town stories, gun-trail stories, ranch stories, an occasional wagon train, railroad, or mining story—and that was about it. Cows and gold and guns. Another memory from those early writing days: I signed my stories W. Ryerson Johnson, influenced by two other western writers, H. Bedford-Jones and S. Omar Barker. We all had common last names and unusual first names, and I thought the single initial in front did something. I later dropped it as being, among other things, redundant.

Street & Smith's *Western Story Weekly* settled down to being my best market, with the company's *Top Notch, Cowboy Stories, Doc Savage,* and *Wild West Weekly* providing dependable sell-off markets. Looking back, that plethora of short story markets doesn't seem real. Some two hundred different magazines flapping their pages in a contest for copy!

There were a few western romance magazines. These straddled the fence, with action and romance intimately entwined. Women were the dominant characters in such magazines as *Rangeland Romances, Thrilling Ranch, Rodeo Romances,* and in the lead magazine of the field, *Ranch Romances*, edited by Fanny Ellsworth.

The large mass of western magazines featured "man action," with women involved only slightly, or not at all. Women were involved in the editing. Notable were Dorothy MacIlwraith at *Short Stories* and Dorothy Hubbard at *Western Story Weekly,* mild-mannered homebody ladies who for many years edited those hard-boiled "man-mags."

Dorothy Hubbard wrote to me once: "Just because your friend, Lloyd Reeve, sometimes puts women in his stories, don't think you have to."

When women were introduced into a story, it was—like the porcupine—carefully, so carefully. There was a cliché understanding that in the action pulps you "cut a woman off at the neck, and didn't bring her back till you got to her knees." Frank Armer's *Spicy Western* was an exception, but even there, very little was explicit, everything suggestive. Rogers Terrill, editor of *Dime Western* at Harry Steeger's Popular Publications, once added a true confession magazine to his list. In a letter he sent out to prospective writers he said: "You know the formula—one part sin and nine parts repentance. With *Candid Confessions* we want you tor reverse the formula." The self-righteous moral majority watchdogs of the day had him off the news-stands with the third issue.

More and more I was working into the longer story lengths. It is easier to plot one 20,000-word novelette than to plot four 5,000-word short stories. In either you build up to one big climactic scene, and you have one set of characters that you shift around in constant conflict or the threat of conflict. In a novelette you have more minor climaxes on the way to the big one—and that's the major difference.

The town-tamer hero was immensely popular in the novelette length. To mention a few: L.L. Foreman had Preacher Devlin, a hellfire and brimstone primitive preacher who would get so riled up at the sin and infamy around him that he'd put his Bible down and help God out a little with righteous blasts from his well-worn six-gun.

Tom Roan had Bullwhip McCrakin—very handy, as you might guess, in bullwhipping a menacing six-gun out of a saloon-bully's hand.

Just maybe influenced by both Preacher and Bullwhip, I worked up a town-tamer series with a character named Len Siringo. Len made his appearance in 30 or so novelettes, most of them printed in Popular Publications' *Star Western*.

Len in every story entered a western town that was helpless in a terror-grip of local gunmen. The gimmick here was that Len entered the scene as a harmless wandering tailor, doctor, printer, grave digger, rainmaker, lightning-rod salesman. . .whatever. During the first part of the story he'd bumble around, and using only the tools of his trade, seem accidentally and miraculously to win in a series of lethal encounters with the criminal gun crew. But somewhere along in the story one of the terrorized locals recognizes him. The whispers go from lip to lip: "This ain't no tailor (doctor, blacksmith, tinker. . .whatnot). This is Len Siringo, the famous gunner for the law who comes in and helps those who can't help themselves." Len rallies the down-hearted beaten locals and in a series of gun-thundering episodes cleans out the killers—and moves on to his next mysterious encounter in another issue of the the magazine.

I worked up another town-tamer of 25-30,000 word "complete novels" featuring Guncat Bodman for *Western Story Weekly*. When he went into a shooting crouch Charley Bodman looked like "a great humped cat." His blue eyes seemed to turn green, and in every story he was characterized as "Charley the Guncat—the man with nine lives to live, and death for six in his trigger finger."

I took a chance one time and developed a series using Wah Lee, a Chinese town-tamer. Instead of six-guns, Wah Lee carried six little "finger knives" which he could flick around faster than a man could draw a gun against him. A Chinese cowboy was so much out of the pattern, I had a bit of a problem selling him. *Western Story Weekly* bought. The series was well received, but that was in 1943 when the pulps were phasing out, and the series didn't last long.

Pulp editors loved alliteration, both in story titles and in the blurbs. In a western story they liked to work in a suggestion of the gun in the title: "Two Guns Tied Low". . ."Lead for the Law". . ."Too Good With Guns". . ."The Town Too Tough To Tame."

Editors sometimes pirated titles. I sold one story called "Bullets For Breakfast." Within the next year or so I saw the title appear in three different magazines.

Alliteration extended to the blurbs that pitched the story to the reader. They were sometimes such a garble of Peter-Piper-picked as to be practically unreadable. One of my Len Siringo novelettes in *Star Western* for example, was retitled "Bullet Chore for a Coffin Drummer," and blurbed: "When a ruthless range-hog's hard-case gun-crew brought a red reign of terror to Ten-Mile Creek, Ben Graves bought in. This coffin drummer extraordinary figured that a goldcamp-gone-wrong as just the proper place to pile up a fortune—even though he himself had to furnish filling for those boot-hill boxes."

One more—blurbing "Bullet Requiem for Len Siringo": "When red terror rode Crazy Creek range, those wronged and desperate ranchers sent for Len Siringo, free-lance gunner for the law. But Big-foot Jimson's greedy gun-crew was already inscribing its own red message for Len—written in the bullet-blasted bodies of honest cowmen!"

It occcurs to me that in these sometimes nitty-gritty, and always telling-it-like-I-found-it reminiscences, I may have given the wrong impression to readers not so familiar with the old western story market. Always there were pulps—and pulps. The best of them—and even occasionally the worst—ran stories that would have fit comfortably between the covers of the high-pay "slicks" magazines such as *Colliers, Saturday Evening Post, Redbook, Liberty, Ladies Home Journal*. . .or the prestigious "quality magazines such as *Harper's, Atlantic*. . . .

Many writers got their start in the pulps. Would you believe Mark Twain, Joseph Conrad, Jack London, Jules Verne, H.G. Wells, Rudyard Kipling, Theodore Dreiser, Arthur Conan Doyle? Add Zane Grey, Dashiell Hammett, Edgar Rice Burroughs, Raymond Chandler, John D. McDonald, Cornell Woolrich, Rider Haggard, Ray Bradbury, and—as a matter of fact, almost all the early science fiction writers. In 1935 Street & Smith's *Top Notch* magazine printed a Silver Anniversary issue in which they listed 66 contributors. Heading the list was President Theodore Roosevelt.

Venerable names were associated with the editing and publishing of pulp magazines. Who remembers today that *Main Street* Nobel Prize winner, Sinclair Lewis, was once assistant editor for Arthur Sullivant Hoffman on *Adventure Magazine?* And H.L. Mencken and George Jean Nathan in 1920 founded and edited *Black Mask.* So a catch prhase, "We don't want it good, we want it Wednesday," didn't necessarily define the quality of the product. It did pretty accurately reflect the speed and quantity of the stories spewing from the presses.

Adios Amigos. . .enjoy this book about those western pulp heroes, and —May your lariat never dig dirt.

INTRODUCTION

You are about to encounter the WESTERN PULP HERO (and maybe even a heroine or two) who rode the dusty trails, each fighting for what he believed in, carrying six-gun justice into a lawless land. It was a time of the gunfighter, bounty hunter, outlaw, renegade Indian. It was a specific moment when the Colt .45 or whatever weapon was hanging by his side became the only law each would live and some would die by.

What then, you may ask, is a western hero? Webster's dictionary tells us that a 'western' is a story, novel, or motion picture dealing with frontier or cowboy life. "Hero' is a person of distinguished valor or fortitude. We have, regrettably, only touched the surface with this endeavor when it comes to surveying those particular individuals who filled the pages of magazines during the 1930s, 1940s, and into the early 1950s.

16

(The actual heyday of all western pulp fiction was from 1930 to late 1940.) Luckily, copies of quite a lot of them have survived. They were as numerous back then as the sands of the Arizona desert. We have managed to cover those found in the Weinberg & McKinstry *Hero Pulp Index*, along with numerous others.

These were selected at random or recommended by some avid western pulp reader. For just one dime, sometimes a little more, a choice could be made any day of the week at your favorite news-stand or corner drug store, all across the country. Perhaps it was a *Wild West Weekly, Western Story, Texas Rangers, Masked Rider, The Range Riders, West, Real Western, The Western Raider, Star Western, Riders of the Range, Exciting Western, Thrilling Western, Red Seal Western, Pioneer Western, Dime Western Magazine, The Rio Kid Western, Rangeland Love, Real Western Romances, Rangeland Sweethearts, Ace-High Western, Fifteen Western Tales, Western Rangers, Cowboy Stories, Frontier Stories, Spicy Western*. Actually the list is much longer. But no matter, each magazine caught the eye like a magnet.

Covers for the most part usually featured scenes of action, often complete with smoking guns and some hombre big as life on center stages. He'd have on a wide sombrero, a dark bandanna tied around his neck, a red or blue shirt, dark trousers tucked into high-heeled boots, and a pair of spurs. On a leather vest was a sheriff's star gleaming brightly in the sunlight.

It was Les Beitz who penned these words back in 1947, in an issue of *True West Magazine*: "Until a scant dozen years ago millions of Americans eagerly devoured the rip-roaring contents of any and every "old" pulp western they could lay their hands on. For the better part of five decades these thrillers provided a literary son-of-a-gun stew and renegade marauders that fairly blasted the lid off the old frontier. Like the West itself, the era has passed. But there are still old westerns lurking around here and there."

In an article titled "Twenty-Five Years of Glory," author J. Edward Leithead remarked: "Stacks of them (westerns) appeared on all news-stands and just as regularly they were bought up."

Richard Wilkinson, a veteran author, said: "A man didn't do a lot of research. Neither the editors nor the readers worried about accuracy, location, or periods. It was just good entertainment."

We asked author Dan Cushman what attracted readers to the western pulps. His response: "They were so much a part of Americana; or are so much. They were aimed at the ordinary joe who came home after a day working in the roundhouse and got his economical kicks out of *Dime Western* rather than the radio."

So beyond all doubt the pulp westerns did ride a trail right into literary history and will never die, but will remain always a part of our American folklore, a segment of our heritage. Characters like Jim Hatfield, Wayne Morgan, Robert Pryor, and even The Shooting Gallery Kid must have had what William J. Bennett wrote about in a *Newsweek Magazine* article: "A largeness of soul; a hitching of their own purposes to larger purposes, to something that demanded endurance or sacrifice or courage or resolution or compassion."

Author Ron Goulart, writing in his excellent book *Cheap Thrills (A History of Pulp Fiction)*, had a slightly different viewpoint: "The writers who rode the pulp range were legion; most are forgotten, their reputation in no better shape today than the crumbling yellow paper on which their stories appeared."

The subject of a single character in the western epics provoked the following comment from two noted pulp connoisseurs, Robert Kenneth Jones and Robert Sampson. Writing in *Echoes Magazine*, Jones said: "In the frenzied world of pulp writing, authors could help their own cause in a simple way. They could create a series character. The public generally liked familiar faces. The editors did, too."

In the noted series "A Time of Lively Fiction," written for *Dime Novel Round Up,* Sampson said: "The several fiction magazines and the more specialized western fiction magazines abound in series characters, all essentially the same figure— a quick-gun artist, laconic, lean, strong on decency and ethical codes."

Author J.P. Guinon had these words: "Many of the best-known fiction writers of the day turned their hand to westerns, and the lovers of such tales had a ball for the next few years. The stuff was decidedly not literature with a capital L in most cases, but it represented imagination and action that kept the average American who reads for entertainment making frequent trips to the news-stand. It was worth it."

Now the time has come for each of you to meet those individuals and the legends that surround their lives. So why not come with me and pause on a wind-swept section of land just beyond some prairie cowtown? Here ashen gray earth is joined by mesquite, prickly pear, soapweed, and scrub oak. Nearby tall cactus gaze silently into the sunlight. Hoofprints cut deep into the dust, surrounded by endless patches of grease weed.

Out of the haze a rider appears. He is tall in the saddle, slender of build and of whipcord strength, eyes a gray-green, simmering quietly.

His face is deeply tanned, mouth firm, nose straight or possibly hawk-like. Strapped low on his hip are a pair of walnut-handled Colt .45's. Now, beyond the rider, a man is seen coming from one of the many false-fronted buildings. Beneath his smoothly-tailored Prince Albert coat are a pair of nickel-plated, pearl-handled six-guns. He know how to use them. He moves into the street and stands there. He waits. His dark eyes glance all around. He sees the Red Bird Saloon, the Undertaker's, the Livery Stable, the Cafe. Dust devils roam the street. Horses stand quietly at nearby hitching rails. The show-down is at hand. It is hero against villain. A grave in "boot hill"—just outside town—awaits the loser. The time is high noon. The time is close to sundown. It makes no difference any-more. . . .

It is Wayne Morgan against Pearly Cooper. It is the Rio Kid versus Duff Gray. It is The Lone Ranger facing Blackjack Malone.

Such are the memories; they serve as the epitaph for all the westerns inscribed on the winds of another moment, engraved forever in glorious color covers. They form a web of all our yesteryears, and we are better for it. Tomorrow may never know them as we have, nor appreciate them as much.

Riders of
the
Gunsmoke Trail

Dade Solo

Maureen Temple

The Silver Buck

THE SILVER BUCK

Western Dime Novels (The Frank A. Munsey Company, a Red Star Magazine, ten cents per issue), published in May of 1940 the first story about the man named above. In July 1940, with the second novel, came a title change to *Red Star Western*. It remained like that with the third story. When the fourth was published in November of 1940, another transformation. It was now *Silver Buck Western*. It stayed like that until the final issue in January, 1941. The titles were:

The Silver Buck.   A Rider without a Range. Valley of the Vanquished.

Plunder Plateau.   Gun Satan of Little Hadies.

Covers and interior art were excellent. The stores were fast-paced, with good dialogue—highly recommended for pulp fans. The author was James Olson.

DADE SOLO was top man, tall, lean, 5 feet 10 inches, straight, blackhaired, with tiny crowsfeet gathering at the corners of his gray-green eyes. Weight was 175. He wore a pair of walnut-gripped .45's, carried in a plain cutaway set of holsters slung close to the hips on a single cartridge belt. He rode a wiry, stubborn roan gelding called WHANG.

His father had been killed by a crooked deputy sheriff. He had been a cattle baron, with a ranch that had a vast range. The elder Solo had gathered various men around him over the years—a Chinese cook, an ex-prize fighter, gunmen, card-sharks. These men taught Dade the trade tricks. For example, the cook instructed him in ju-jitsu and a few other moves: Solo raised his left hand, his fingers spreading behind a person's ear, his thumb jamming into it. The man's eyes rolled back and set themselves with the whites showing. "Hurts until it paralyzes you," Solo remarked. "You'll have an earache for a few hours."

Solo developed a habit of toying with a silver dollar, making it vanish and then leap startlingly into view again. Solo's mother, a former teacher, had taught her son well. He could play both piano and guitar. The mother died shortly after the father was killed. Then Dade joined up with a carnival, worked with magicians, rode in a Wild West Show. Finally he returned to his range in Bound Basin. The Solo ranch was now about twelve hundred acres. With Solo rode young Bill Temple, son of a nearby rancher, Tom Temple. That same rancher had a daughter, MAUREEN, Solo's girl. Old man Temple had been injured two months earlier on the range.

Maureen Temple was "never a timid girl or one to worry foolishly." She had blue eyes, a pert nose, and bronze-colored hair. The two were in love. But then trouble erupted as Solo was framed for the murder of Bill Temple by a crooked lawman. He was eventually sentenced to hang at state prison. As he was being transported by train along with another prisoner, Joe Border, the two made a break for freedom and ended up in a long cabin belonging to an old-timer named PAP RHEEM. When Solo got a chance to see himself in a mirror, he gasped.

He had a bone-deep cut from eye to chin, a beard, and his hair was gray at the temples. His face had changed, making him seem ten years older than his 28 years. In time those wounds healed, but left an angry scar, giving Solo an expression of hard and stolid placidity. He grew a short-cropped mustache, which like his hair was streaked with gray. "His eyes were now a clouded, unfathomable gray, sparkling green when his hatred of the sheriff who framed him, and his separation from Maureen, became thoughts uppermost in his mind."

Solo talked to Pap about revenge on those "who done him wrong." He said: "I have it!" He held up a silver dollar. "I'll make the sign of a silver dollar sicken every buzzard in Bound Basin before I'm through."

From that moment on his name became—The Silver Buck. "I'll need some sort of disguise," he added. "Something that'll rawhide hell out of anybody seeing you," Pap cut in. "That's it," Solo replied, "a rawhide mask." That mask was described as follows: "A rawhide mask had taken the shape of his face, little by little. The part that covered Silver Buck's upper lip stuck out like teeth protruding from a skull. He indented wrinkles at this point, making it look like teeth. He'd built out the cheeks, sunk the eye-holes, worked soot into the hide around his eye sockets. With the mask on, he looked like a desert-dried body, his eyes gleaming through the holes."

The fitted mask covered his face back to the edge of his upper lip. When he spoke, his lower jaw seemed to wag up and down, giving the impression of a skeleton opening and closing its mouth. Later on he told Pap: "I'm beginning to understand this business of a dual personality a little better." (A dual personality is defined as a condition of disordered unconsciousness in which the person leads two lives alternately. It is a mental function which allows a person to maintain an awareness of his immediate environment.)

Between Border and Pap they came up with an outfit for Solo, and a set of guns. (It seemed Pap had a hombre at a nearby trading post who did some work on a set of weapons.) Then the old man gave Solo "a slew of silver dollars." By now there was a five thousand dollar reward for Solo, along with a thousand for Joe Border and five hundred for the recovery of the bodies or for information about them.

"Yuh see, Border," said Solo, "why it's best the Silver Buck rides alone." Thus did the Silver Buck head for the owlhoot trails, wanted for a crime he was innocent of. He hunted for the two men who could clear his name. He was a confident, muscular figure in dust-covered gray pants, shirt, and hat. He had a blanket-lined canvas coat. He let his hands dangle near a pair of walnut-handed .45's. He wore full, high-heeled boots. One item he carried in his boot was a "bit of flat steel spring," used for such things as opening padlocks and handcuffs.

Here is a quick look at the Silver Buck in action: "Silver Buck stepped in quickly, weaved suddenly as Nig struck clumsily out at him and got his hands on the back of Nig's thick neck. The big man screamed at the top of his lungs as he went to his knees. He continued to scream as Silver Buck gripped his neck, pressing on the nerves that sent torturing pains of hell through Nig's body.

STREET AND SMITH'S

WESTERN STORY

MAGAZINE • JAN. 27, 1940

THE RED X BRAND
Book length novel by W. Ryerson Johnson
and many other stories

GUNCAT BODMAN

The above magazine, *Western Story*, featured Guncat Bodman, a character from the pen of author Ryerson Johnson.

Charles Bodman was a town-tamer of the first water. His reputation was that of a top gun. He was a roll-your-own smoker and always shaved himself. He'd let a barber cut his hair, but that was all. His stomping grounds were from border to border. He was a man who walked slowly, with a peculiar springy, almost feline gait. A pleasant-looking man, body long and lean, with mild blue eyes, hair the color of sand, which brushed his forehead in a curly tangle. He had an intelligent-looking forehead, lean face, square-cut jaw, and easy grin. His face was brown and leathery from exposure to desert sun and wind. There was a bullet burn on the side of his jaw—a slight scar, roughly in the shape of a star. He would sometimes carry a pocket watch on a chain with an ornamental bullet of silver. He was able to read Morse code. He was a master at the gun trade. He knew precisely what he could do with a gun and what he could not do. A resourceful man when in a tight corner indeed. Once when in jail, he "loosened one boot, extracted a stubby-bladed knife from between the leather and his sock." Also, now and then he would carry another weapon in a shoulder holster. In addition, he had a tobacco sack filled with lead pellets.

"Don't you ever get tired of being a kind of unofficial executioner?" a woman asked him once. "You got your terms mixed up, ma'am," he said. "An executioner kills somebody who's helpless to resist. Mostly I think he gets some fun from killin'. It's no fun for me. And them times I've had to kill, I've done it shootin' into somebody else's gun. I've done it to save many lives."

(Life, he reasoned, was as sweet to another man as it was to him.) He had this philosophy where women were concerned: "Women were the devil. Worse than either gold or lead when it comes to mixing a man's life up." He also had these comments: "I hate killin'. But I came here this morning to kill four men. I've killed 'em. I killed 'em because in a new land where there's always elbow room for all, they robbed other men of the very air they breathed. I killed 'em so other men could live."

Charlie "Guncat" Bodman--the man with nine lives and death for six in his trigger finger. The title had been given to him when he first started throwing lead for the law. He was "the youngest marshal west of Dodge City, Kansas." As a frontier lawman for one hell-raising town after another, he fed on danger. It was in every breath he took. And he had disciplined his body to respond to his will. It was one reason he had lived so long. His six-gun magic was another. Because of this a tradition of nine-life invincibility had been built up about him.

His ability with a gun is demonstrated as follows: As he was about to draw, he went into a fast catlike crouch posture, and in those few telling seconds, his eyes glittered and seemed to blaze with a pale–green cast, pupils squeezed to thin black marks, lips thinned to parchment against his teeth. The gun-draw was almost always the same, although sometimes he didn't go into the famous cat-crouch. The draw—all forearm and wrist movement.

Only a few of the more alert onlookers were even aware of that. But every man there was aware of the six-gun once it had cleared leather.

Here is another: The Guncat, crouching, had his own gun cleared from leather, and his lead blazed in return. It came so fast and it came straight. The bullet tore Fessby's chest, seeming to club him backwards. His body on the bunk stiffened, then relaxed in a way a live body never does. Charlie Bodman blew smoke from his gun and holstered it.

Once, forced to play William Tell, he shot a potato right from a young boy's head: Bodman faced the boy, his muscles relaxed, face calm. His voice came soothingly, gentle and confident: "Easy, Frankie. Just stand upright and still." Then before the boy knew it, Bodman was ready. He leveled up and fired. The bullet smashed the potato from the boy's head. It happened so fast the onlookers felt cheated.

Here is a sequence from "One More Town To Tame," November 24, 1942 issue:

"The Guncat!" the Professor gasped.

"Unless you want it to be a dyin' revelation, drop your gun!"

"Drop whose gun?' the other snarled. "I'm cold-beadin' you, same as you are me. My chances are as good as yours."

"Maybe so your chances are. But your nerves ain't. I'm countin'. When I say "Three" you want to have that gun dropped."

"If you blast me you'll dig your own grave. My bead's as good as yours."

"Here's countin." The Guncat laughed with his lips tight across his teeth. "One. . .Two. . .He never said 'three.'" The Professor let his gun drop. It whacked loudly against the floor.

We found this descriptive passage in "Trail of the Golden Horseshoe," November 8, 1941: He rode into the gold camp around noon. Hostile glances followed him. Not that he was recognized, but his type was. His low-slung gun, something about the way he carried himself in the saddle—the easy confidence, the hint of arrogance even—marked him for the breed of man who ran the West, who rode where he pleased, and used his gun if necessary.

One thing about Guncat Bodman was this: He was always wanting, always trying to settle down. He wanted to find a place to hang up his wide-brimmed sombrero. But he never quite seemed to make it. There was always just one more gun job a little further west. "Been lookin' all my born days, seems like, for a chance to chuck my guns and hunker down somewhere. But every time I've picked me out a gal, and a place to settle in, I get a call to go trouble-gunnin' at some place where men and women have already settled and are just findin' out the West is still wild."

Author John Dinan said this about Ryerson Johnson: "Johnson's westerns read smoothly and easily. His dialogue was in the terse and tough *Black Mask* style. Johnson was an excellent story-teller who could deliver believable action stories."

There is a particular paragraph in "Trail of the Golden Horseshoe," in which the author described a specific gunman engaged in a fight with the Guncat: Keno Cane was another who didn't quit. The gun boss, with his pack being licked six ways from Sunday, stood his ground, six-shooter blazing. His face was white, his lips bloodless. The smoke of battle roiled about his black string tie, against his white short front, about his plum-colored coat and polished boots. He looked as oddly neat and immaculate as though he were sitting in the Golden Sawdust saloon at his own gambling table, where the smoke that reeked about him was from tobacco instead of gunpowder.

Ryerson Johnson had the following description which to a westerner like myself speaks so eloquently: In the West the sun bedded down in a vast sea of grass. It was an angry red sun that looked hot enough to ignite the dried grass. But it merely sent fiery streaks halfway around the sky—hot colors, blazing red, orange, purple, that spoke of violence. Then the sun was gone and the moon was there, a cool white disc making a thing of beauty out of even so ordinary a growth as a cholla cactus. The Guncat burned a cigarette down to his lips, then ground the glowing end under his heel. Around him were the night noises, the rasp and peeping of insects, and distinctly, the sad, nerve-tingling cry of a coyote.

Hopalong Cassidy's Western Magazine, Fall 1950. Success of his television program brought forth a new series of Cassidy's adventures written by Louis L'Amour.

HOPALONG CASSIDY

When many of us hear the above name our thoughts do not go atutomatically to the pulp western. Instead we see in our mind's eye William Boyd, white-haired, dressed in black, astride a white horse. This was the motion-picture image. In the bloody pulps he was a character entirely different—at first. Unfortunately, we have seen only two issues of the stories and therefore recommend that any Cassidy fan read Robert Sampson's book, *Yesterday's Faces,* the first volume, and a chapter titled "Forty Miles South, Near the Pecos." Meanwhile we will attempt to take a mini-look at a most remarkable figure. On our desk is a copy of *Argosy All-Story Weekly,* dated May 2, 1925. (The cover reproduced above.) This has a first-part story by Clarence E. Mulford. In this one Cassidy talks like this: "Buck, it ain't yore fool idear that every man's honest. If you had any reason to believe that way, it wouldn't be so bad; but you've been buttin' ag'in cattle thieves all yore life, an' you shore oughta know better by this time."

Some pages later: "Hopalong turned like a flash, two guns appearing in his big hands. The movement had been so quick that it found the crowd unprepared, their thoughts too self-centered on what they were prepared to do. "Just practicin'," he explained with a grin, but there was something in his poised attitude that kept every man present from making any mistakes.

Next we found *The Hopalong Cassidy Western Magazine.* The hero is described as one with "cold blue eyes." He wore silver-plated six-shooters, with bone handles gleaming white, their balance perfect. His draw was like greased lightning and was demonstrated in the first story: Neither man saw the blur of movement as Hopalong drew. His guns came up, spouting flames even as they cleared leather, and his first shot was for the tall man, whom he had rightly deduced was the more dangerous of the two. The shot hit just above the glistening gun belt. In almost the same instant Hopalong's other gun roared, and the younger man went to his knees. He tried a shot that tugged at Cassidy's sleeve, then spilled over in the dust, loosening his grip on the pistols. (The story was called "Rustlers of West Fork.")

COMPLETE WESTERN BOOK *Magazine*

2 NEW NOVELS

BLACK TRAIL OF THE GUN DAMNED by L. R. SHERMAN

OWLHOOT OUTCAST by PETER DAWSON

WILD BUNCH GUN MEDICOS by ED EARL REPP

THE BLACK DEATH

This character has to be one of the most unique in pulp western fiction. I simply had to include him. The author: L.R. Sherman. The magazine: *Complete Western Book* (a Red Circle magazine, cost: 15 cents). The issue: August of 1938. The story: "Black Trail of the Gun Damned."

The hero is an avenger known as The Black Death. One gambling man said about him: "An eagle on the trail of his prey."

His real name was CURT PRESTON, riding a ten-year vengeance trail to avenge his parents' death. That incident had taken place years earlier on their home ranch. Curt had been sixteen years of age when night riders, all of them masked, struck the Circle Star ranch and burned it to the ground. His father and mother shot to death, the ranch foreman left bleeding to death—young Curt vowed right then to get even somehow. Ten powder-stained years with but a single excuse for his existence had made him into a "nerveless, cold-blooded, merciless gunman." His real task lay in the town of Shinbone. Riding out of Durango with two companions (both very savage) also came violence, bloodshed and death.

Curt was tall, lean-hipped, angular and powerful looking, with sun-darkened face and gray eyes. There was a smooth confidence in very lithe movement. Tight grim lines habitually scored his face. Clad in black, he wore a low-crowned, wide-brimmed Stetson, and spurless half-boots. Suspended from crossed cartridge belts, two black holsters, shining dully with oil, held twin forty-fours, huge, heavy-framed guns with eight-inch barrels. Saddle, stirrup leather, saddle-bags, and bridle were also black. His two companions were Niger and Satan, a magnificent coal-black stallion, and a huge black cougar. Both horse and cougar responded to a short, piercing whistle. Once this was given, the cougar would sink to the ground, "yellow eyes fastened on its master; the stallion became a statue in black." Then, as Preston swung into the saddle, he made a motion with his hand to the cougar. It ran ahead of the horse, disappearing with a noiseless, padded tread. (Preston had found the cougar as a sprawling, half-starved kitten, and had nursed and trained it.)

Two women were involved with the The Black Death. One was Elsa Tanner; the other, named Daisy, worked in a saloon. It was Daisy who told Preston: "I think I'm going to like you a lot. Either that or I'm going to hate you like hell. I'm going to make you like me, too. You're a man."

Preston was given some aid by a Chinese named Hip Long, introduced to him by one Kee Lo (whose father had cooked on the Circle Star ranch). Lo and Preston had been children together. Hip Long turned out to be a first-class fighting man. "I shall be glad to fight by your side. Should you need them, I pray you will accept this unworthy one's services," he said.

A description of Preston: Then Preston watched for nearly a quarter of an hour, and while he watched, he became once again The Black Death. All traces of softness were erased from his thoughts: the granite exterior shell he presented to the world seemed to deepen and harden. His mouth was a tight line, the eyes slitted and gray and cold.

Here we see some action: His disengaged right hand hung loosely at his side, the fingers barely touching the leather of his holsters. The cold, merciless stare of the man swept the entire room. The slitted gray eyes missed nothing. "When approaching a trap," he once explained, "I always do it with my eyes open. When I approach a brace of skunks I do it with my eyes closed, but when a couple of coyotes cross my path I sometimes, by way of warning, do this-" There was a flashing double movement of his right hand. In the midst of the movement the room rocked with two thunderous explosions. Then Preston stood as before, with hands hanging idly by his filled hoster. The bartender could have sworn that the right gun of the black-clad man had not left leather, yet the gun hands of the two men challenging him had jerked to their heads, and blood trickled between their fingers. (Preston also kept a knife hidden at a spot between his shoulder blades.)

We also have this sequence: The big hands of Solveski flashed down at his six-gun. Preston moved with practiced ease, with blinding speed, and with preconceived purpose. His first shot punctured Solveski's arm, and the second and third shots plowed into the big torso just above the belt buckle.

Solveski's first lead cut into the floor at his feet. He jerked to the impact of the black rider's fire, then charged cursing and reaching across with his left hand to secure the gun from his useless right. Preston fired again, and then a fifth time, and leaped back. Solveski, blood bubbling from his lips, kept coming. He forced up the gun in his left hand. Preston's left hand twitched and flame leaped from it. A little black hole appeared in Solveski's face, just above the bridge and nose. He pitched forward and down, still trying to thumb the hammer of his gun by reflex action when all consciousness was blocked out in the midnight that was death.

This singular western pulp may be hard to find after all these years, but if it comes your way, don't toss it aside. The Black Death and his two "companions" will give you some mighty good reading and lots of action.

WHITE EAGLE

Big Chief Western (a Red Star magazine) of The Frank A. Munsey Company, price ten cents, with the October 1940 issue gave us the first column about White Eagle—"mightiest of Comanche braves." The author: Arthur Lawson. The cover artist was not identified. Interior art, by V.E. Pyles, was very well done.

"Let the drums thunder as tribute to him—this blond Comanche brave, mightiest warrior of the west. With his bow and his battle ax he sets out on a perilous trail—to defend the honor of his tribe against the white man's, which he disowned."

It was said of White Eagle that he could "shave the whiskers off a frog at twenty paces with an ax and not even frighten the frog. Then with a war arrow he could cut off the frog's tail without drawing blood."

White Eagle was described as tall, well over six feet, and broad in the shoulders, slender of hips, with a lean strong face. His skin was smooth and brown, with eyes a deep blue. He moved with an easy grace and had a quick, boyish smile. He could throw a tomahawk with great skill, but preferred a hatchet or ax. His ability with a bow and arrow was uncanny. When first seen by Dallas Reade, "he was taller than any Indian and he moved with a kind of grace that was somehow different."

In the very beginning he was not yet a brave, but this soon changed as he underwent the torture that all of the young men of the tribe must go through. Then he was truly White Eagle, Comanche warrior. His Indian mother was called by the name of Hahteen.

His number one companion throughout all the adventures was NO THUNDER, son of Big Buffalo (as was White Eagle). He was a Comanche of average height, slender, powerfully built, with black hair and obsidian eyes. He was White Eagle's friend and stood by him through thick and thin.

The girl in all of this turmoil was DALLAS READE, daughter of Mike Reade, a small ranch owner. She was slim, lithe, and her bare arms and legs were pale as bleached buckskin. Her face was a delicate oval, but there was strength in the set of her small jaw. She held her head proudly. "Her eyes are the color of deep water and her hair is sunlight"—so spoke No Thunder.

The first novel is full of constant, swift-moving action. In one particular sequence No Thunder was wounded. They were trying to climb a trail up the side of a canyon. The bullet had cut No Thunder's hand. He could not hold on. "Let me take you on my shoulders," White Eagle told his companion. White Eagle climbed close to No Thunder, bracing himself tightly against the wall. Then No Thunder let himself down as far as his good hand would allow. Here his legs were on White Eagle's back, reaching almost to the waist. He let go. When he caught White Eagle's shoulder the sudden stop nearly jerked the bigger man off the cliff. White Eagle grunted and hung on. He started climbing again with the burden on his back. When he reached the ledge No Thunder had spoken of, he gripped his brother with his free arm so that No Thunder would not try to stay behind. A huge boulder hurtled down, bouncing from the face of the cliff. White Eagle put the last of his great strength into that terrible climb. With one arm he pulled himself over the rim. He lowered No Thunder to the ground, and then stood a moment, his wide chest heaving as he took long, steady breaths. His eyes were bright with triumph.

White Eagle

HAPPY-HAY

"I'm not a gunman. I'm just a hoss-trader, and I'm not even a good hoss-trader."

That's what he told 'em, folks. But don't you for one second believe it. He built up a reputation where horses were concerned. His epic adventures were penned by W.C. Tuttle in *New Western Magazine*.

His real name was Happy "Tom" Hay, and one hombre remarked, "Seems to me I heard of him up here in Kansas. 'Bout the best damned shot with a Colt or a saddle gun anybody ever seen, I hears."

Happy Hay was always getting himelf mixed up in some kind of trouble where horses were concerned. He explained why this way: "I reckon I jumped the crick 'fore I came to the bridge, like I'm always doin'." He was past thirty years of age, very tall and angular, plain rather than handsome, but he had a frank, open countenance, a cheerful grin and white teeth, steady blue eyes. He wore a really big sombrero, blue shirt, old-style chaps with fringed sides. His boots were extra high of heel. Around his waist he wore a homemade cartridge belt, and looped into it was a homemade holster with an old Frontier Colt .45.

He happened to be one man who found beauty in a panorama of hills and range untouched by man. He had an interesting outlook on life and other things: "It's always been my idea that sidewinders an' other snakes, human or animal, should be stomped on wherever found." Here's another: "When a man's only got sixty-seven years to look at so much that's purty, it's funny how some men spend all their lives diggin' and scrapin' just to rake together more money than they got any use for."

On the other hand, when it came to the female of the species, Happy Hay really told 'em: "You hosses is like wimmin. The prettier you are, the more trouble you git into." We better mention three of his horses. There was a sorrel he rode named Powder, another called Buzz, and one named Rattler. "A child could handle Buzz,' he explained once, "but no man except me has ever rode Rattler. He'd kill yuh. He's killed men. He's my watch dog, only better." Whenever Hay wanted to summon Rattler, all he had to do was "put his fingers to his mouth, whistle three times. An unusual shrill whistle."

Now let's take a look at Happy in action: "I wouldn't go monkeyin' with that gun if I were you," said Happy Hay friendly-like as he watched the man's hairy right hand swing back, fingers dangling over the butt of the holstered gun at his hip. "Yuh wouldn't do what?" the enraged man glared. His hand dropped like a flash, jerking the gun loose from the leather. Then with deceiving smoothness Hay moved. One moment his hand was by his side—empty. The next instant it somehow charmed a gun out of thin air. The gun flashed. Hawkins felt the shock of pain—and found himself staring dazedly at his own gun spinning on its cylinder a dozen feet away on the sidewalk. His hand was numb and the knuckles bleeding.

Here is one more: "You killed him because he claimed the cards were marked?" Happy said.

"That's what happened."

"Well," Happy said slowly, "he was right. They've been marked by a gambler who deals seconds. They're thumb-marked."

The gambler's eyes widened as if in amazement that anyone should make such a statement. Then they narrowed again to deadly slits. "You lie!"

"I don't lie," said Happy, "and," he smiled slowly, "that pocket killer of yours only shoots one shell. Have yuh got another of them murder guns in yore pocket or do yuh murder just one man a day?"

The gambler stared at him, saying nothing. Only his nostrils quivered, his lips tightened until the teeth threatened to cut the flesh. The black-coated follower at his shoulder started to make a movement—and then stopped. Happy Hays' glance, as quick as a hawk's, had turned that way. And there was no longer a smile in the blue eyes.

A final glimpse of Happy Hay: Ace Hudson made his move. His hand darted up for the breast of his coat. Happy's hand shot down for the gun in his waistband. "Yore mistake, Ace! But it'll be the last one yuh ever make!" Almost together the two guns spoke. The lock of hair at the side of Happy's head lifted, and a faint line of red sprang up where the gambler's bullet had seared its way past. But the gambler himself staggered, opened his mouth. A look of amazement and then horror spread over his face. He glanced down dazedly at the spot of red that had suddenly appeared on his white shirt front. Even as he looked, it glistened and spread. Then slowly the gambler's knees began to sag under him. Sagged until with a shudder that seemed to shake his whole body, Ace Hudson suddenly crumpled up and fell, the short-barrel pistol dropping from his loosened fingers as he fell. He twitched once, and lay still.

POTLUCK JONES

The above magazine *(Western Story)* featured a character by the name of Potluck Jones (pictured above right), from the pen of Ney N. Greer. This unique individual rode the trails with a sidekick known as "Too-Bad" Tommy O'Neil. It seems the two of them were raised together after Potluck was found in a covered wagon that had stopped near a dry water hole. Both parents were dead. He got the name of Jones because that's what had been printed on the side of the covered wagon. Brought into the family circle, Tommy's father said of him: "He can take potluck along with the rest of us." So he grew up on the ranch, working the cattle, riding rimrock and cedar brakes. Tommy and Potluck used "signs" between themselves which were of their own invention and meaningless to anyone else. So, as time went on, Too-Bad and Potluck became inseparable. They became known as "a pair of lucky lawmen, quick on the trigger and rough on rats. Bad medicine for bad men." Both had influential friends such as the governors of two states, and once their pictures appeared in the *Denver Telegraph* newspaper.

Potluck developed an "eye" for the female sex. For instance, in one story, "Potluck Picks A Trail," July 31, 1937, he was really taken with a gal named Wanda. "You're so danged beautiful," he told her, "just to look at you makes my heart turn handsprings in my throat." But it was up to O'Neil to keep him in check. Adventure called—not romance, so Too-Bad never let Potluck "peg his pony too long on any one range."

As Too-Bad said: "Potluck, I shore wish you'd get yore mind off the gals. Yuh keep me in hot water most of the time."

Potluck was honest, frank and open, loyal to the core, unstinting with his friends. "The voice of the guns and the intimate whisper of passing lead were not new to him. He had always taken gunfighting with a serious turn of mind. Life was pleasant and worth living, and one bullet could put an end to all that. When in the saddle he usually rode a chestnut gelding.

Potluck had a couple of favorite weapons. One was a keen-as-a-razor sheath knife. And he loved his ivory-handled, gold-mounted Colt .45's, sometimes carrying just one, other times two weapons.

From an early story comes this: His keen eyes on the bandit leader, Potluck let his hammer fall. His shot blended with the belching thunder of Tommy's guns. Death snatched the hindmost—those slow or unsteady with their triggers. The outlaw leader staggered and Potluck smashed a second, then a third slug into him. Tommy's blue eyes sparkled. His guns bucked high and fast.

Potluck was a lawman to the core, and his trail-hardened body carried the marks of wounds which only in time would heal completely. He had the avid curiosity of a pine squirrel, which often got him into trouble. He was young, tall, lithe, with sun-tanned features, a clean-cut boyish face, light brown, moody eyes, a powerful frame, wide shoulders, with strong arms and supple fingers. He had this bit of philosophy: "No honorable man is ever quite dead. Some part of him lingers on to become the driving power of those who follow him."

Potluck's friend, TOMMY "TOO-BAD" O'NEIL, was small of body, with a pug-nosed and freckled face, blue eyes, red hair, slender hips, and short, saddle-curved legs. An amused grin made his lean, sun-tanned face look boyish. He seemed especially to like anything mechanical. He rode a big roan horse. He wore twin Colts, silver-mounted .45 caliber guns with silver-inlaid butts, on a wide belt. One other item was a set of bat-wing chaps heavy with silver conchos. He often said: "Here today, gone tomorrow, hitting the high spots like a tumbleweed. Seems like wherever me and Potluck light, it's sandy soft and we can't take root."

In the story "Potluck Picks A Trail," he happened to enter a cave in the side of a cliff. Here is a short sequence: His scalp prickled; his eyes bulged. Complete in every detail, human skeletons surrounded him on all sides. They stood erect in motionless repose, leering at him through vacant eye sockets. They were grotesquely outlined and clearly visible in the pitchy darkness by a ghostly phosphorescent glow. As Potluck's bulging eyes slowly circled the room, one skeleton took on movement behind him. Its rattling bones furnished a sort of dry, satanic music to which the other skeletons kept time in a gibbering dance of death. Potluck flinched and sprang away, beyond the reach of those clutching hands.

Potluck had, it seemed, been taking lessons in ventriloquism, while at the same time Too-Bad Tommy was taking instruction in ju-jitsu. Tommy told Potluck: "Ju-jitsu is the coming thing! The human body is full of nerves. A sudden pressure in the right place and—I'm just learning." (You can read all about it in the July 11, 1942 issue.)

Here is a final glimpse of Potluck: He was walking down the street of a Mexican town. There was nothing peculiar about his tall, slender frame. He was dressed in tight-fitting Levis, sun-faded blue cotton shirt, a nondescript vest which was buttoned, its upper vest pocket bulging with cigar wrappers. He wore a pair of costly Texas riding boots and a gray, flat-crowned sombrero. A braided leather throat cord on the hat dangled freely under his lean and strong-boned jaw. His sun-bronzed, smoothly shaven face was rigidly set. He had a wide and generous mouth.

Bud Jones of Texas

From the August 13, 1927 issue.

by J. Allan Dunn

The magazine: *Wild West Weekly*. The author: Allan Dunn. Here is a character I knew very little about until Lester Belcher called my attention to him. Bud was at one time another of those gents known as Texas Rangers.

We first meet Bud in Kansas, somewhere west of Dodge City, where he worked as a farm choreboy. His father had been killed by the fall of a steel rail while working on the railroad with a construction gang. His mother had died during his infancy. He was now aged 18, two inches below six feet tall, strong and supple, lean and hard-muscled. His face was tanned, eyes clear and steady, a good mouth and a firm chin. He could ride a horse, shoot, and follow a trail pretty good. His one big ambition was to become a full-fledged Texas Ranger. Bud was able to hook up with a family by the name of Hutchinson, who were headed for the Lone Star State. In due time they reached Kimble County, Texas, and settled down. It was there Bud first met up with a company of Rangers headed by one Captain Halstead, a grizzled fifty-year-old veteran. They were in the area to carry out a roundup of outlaws, seaching in particular for one "Red" Mervin. There was a five-hundred dollar reward on Mervin's head. There were twenty-eight Rangers in Halstead's troop. When Bud asked to join up, the captain said: "You're young yet. Besides, I haven't got a vacancy in the troop."

"If I caught Mervin, would you let me join up?"

"I'll do what I can for you, son."

In short order the Rangers spotted Mervin, hiding out in the cedar brakes up on Turkey Mountain. But he was able to elude them. Bud Jones took out after him. One Ranger had been killed by the outlaw. Bud found the owlhoot: "Stick 'em up, Red! Hoist 'em and keep 'em that way!" The outlaw stiffened. Bud went on: "Drop yore pistol. Jerk it over the bluff to the crick. No monkey business. You're worth jest as much dead as alive." Naturally it wasn't going to be that easy, even though Mervin had been wounded earlier by another Ranger. "You got me, kid," he said. But a moment later Bud found himself thrown from his feet. Mervin was on top of him, forty pounds heavier, a powerful, desperate man. Suddenly the tables were turned. Bud was fighting for his life. In the end, he did come out the winner. "Do I join up?" he asked the captain. "There's a vacancy, and if you don't get it, it won't be my fault," came the reply.

So at this time Bud went on probation, having served about three weeks. Because of the reward money paid on Mervin, he was able to purchase a horse, a Winchester rifle and a bowie knife. Nobody there considered him a tenderfoot. The Rangers were still in Kimble County. This time they were after a gent named McCabe. With this McCabe was his wife and son. The Rangers found out where the wife was living. "You came to us looking like a country boy," the head of the Rangers told Bud. "I want you to look like that again. Go to McCabe's cabin and get all the information you can. You're not spying on a woman, Bud. This is war. War against crime. She and the boy will be better off without McCabe."

Bud found the cabin. In time, however, he was taken prisoner, caught by one of the outlaws who said: "H'ist yore hands, thar! H'ist em!" They dragged Bud before the outlaw chief. "I've a mind to slit yore throat. You're a spy, that's what you are, sir!"

"Better heave him over the cliff, Mac," one outlaw said.

"I'll skin him alive. Tie him up. Link Dodge'll be erlong soon an' he saw this feller ridin' with those troopers two days ergo. We'll wait."

They bound Bud hand and foot and fastened the rope to a nearby tree. It sure looked like the end for him. But there was one thing—the outlaws had overlooked his knife! Bud worked himself free, the outlaws were captured, and McCabe was killed. So Bud was really winnin' his spurs.

Next we've got Lester Belcher's outline on one particular Bud Jones yarn he thought everybody should hear about. It seems that Jones was sent after another outlaw who had fled into Mexico. The Mexican soldiers stopped Bud and would not allow him to cross. So all Bud could do was camp on one side of the Rio Grande and wait. Bud got hungry for something other than "sow belly" and he decided to do something about that, at least. He set a big heavy cord with a large hook on one end, and tied it to a bush by the side of the river. He hoped to catch a real big catfish. A big one grabbed it and yanked Bud right into the Rio Grande, and hauled him right to the Mexican side, where the soldiers nabbed him and the catfish. They pulled him right out of the water. But, instead of gunplay, they decided to skin that catfish and join forces for a feast. They told Jones—"Hang the outlaw. Let's be friends."

Belcher told me: "Bud Jones is a real good character. He deserves to be included." If our luck holds out, maybe Lester will find us a few more adventures to read.

From the August 20, 1927 issue.

Outlaws of Buzzards' Roost
(A Bud Jones of Texas Story)
by J. Allan Dunn

There were only three issues of the magazine pictured above, published by Dell Publishing Company, Inc. By today's standards they are very rare indeed. The dates in question: November of 1936; July and September of 1937.

Each issue contained the story of a particular Jones film. These were, respectively: *The Boss Rider of Gun Creek; Left-Handed Law, and Smoke Tree Range.*

The magazine covers, two of which were identified as sketched by Sidney Riesenberg, caught the eyes immediately. Particularly outstanding was the one showing Buck Jones, gun in hand, sitting astride his white horse, Silver. Each issue held a personal message from the film star under the title of "Greetings from the Range." In one, he wrote: "My business is to make cowboy motion pictures just as real as I can and true to life as I know it is lived on the range—and everywhere else for that matter." Every issue had a complete novel, two novelettes and a series of short stories, written by such authors as Gunnison Steele, Victor Kaufman, and William F. Bragg.

In his book *Yesterday's Faces,* author Robert Sampson wrote: "In 1936 the *Buck Jones Western* failed to cash in on the Buck Jones name."

When Jones died in that California fire in November of 1942, we "lost one of our greatest western film stars. Many people believed his popularity went beyond that of Ken Maynard, Tom Mix, and even Tim McCoy." I know one thing—I enjoyed his films, especially those Rough Rider series he made with McCoy and Raymond Hatton for Monogram Pictures. But I also liked to read *Buck Jones Western Stories.*

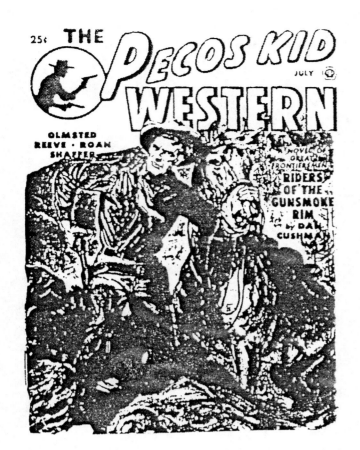

The Pecos Kid

THE PECOS KID

It was a great magazine while it lasted—for five issues. Published bi-monthly by Recreational Reading, Inc., the cost was twenty-five cents. It was undoubtedly among the finest series to be found in the pulps. To any western connoisseur who at some distant point in his or her past walked among the places mentioned, it carried still more meaning. For others, each novel brought vividly to life a part of the West they never knew. The author was Dan Cushman, a very prolific writer. He wrote these words to me: "I wrote a couple of million words for the pulps, under my own name and various house names." Concerning the Pecos Kid stories, he said: "I received a request from Mr. Mike Tilden, then at Popular Publications, to do a series, and the main thing I recall during the period it was published was that I always delayed doing the next one until Mike started to telegraph me ("Please, if you can't send story now, send resumé so illustrations can be made," etc.) and that way he was less likely to reject the copy or ask for a lot of alterations."

The cover depicted above was by Norman Saunders. The stories were titled: "Riders of the Gunsmoke Rim," July 1950; "Three for the Deadwood Drive," September 1950; "Raiders of the Stage Trails," January 1951; "Tamers of the Deadfall Towns," March 1951; and "Buckaroos of the Big Die," June 1951.

The Kid's name was WILLIAM CALHOUN WARREN, an unruly, blue-eyed, brick-red-haired, quick-tempered son of the saddle. His philosophy: "I'm an old rabble soldier in search of my fortune. Sometimes a man turns up and wants to shoot me. I have them buried all the way from here to San Sabe. After a man's roots are tore up he gets to looking for something without knowing what it is, and pretty soon he's put a thousand miles of grass under him. Nothing smells good but the country over the next horizon. I'm not looking for trouble. And I'll give you warning right now. Next one, if I'm lucky enough to outdraw him, is going to need more'n a bonesetter. He's going to need a man with a shovel." One woman told him: "I heard you were the fastest gunman who ever came north of Wyoming."

"They speeded me up a little," he replied. He was a native of the Lone Star State who joined up to fight with the Confederacy during the War Between the States. He served in Tully's Brigade Cavalry, Army of the Mississippi and reached the rank of major in 1864. Three years of fighting made a man of him.

His father, after lying about his age, also joined the Confederacy. He was killed at Pea Ridge. Warren had one brother, a full colonel of cavalry who served under Stirling Price in Missouri. He also died. There were no other children. His mother, never identified, died during the first year of the war. Following the end of the conflict Warren returned to Texas, but found his old ranch in ruins, everything destroyed. There was a gal who had waited for him, but somehow now things were different and it never worked out. So he took to the frontier trails. He worked for a time with the Arkansas Stockman's Federation, running down cattle rustlers. He was now pictured as follows: Slim, six feet tall, one hundred and sixty pounds of muscle, a long lean jaw, and twenty-eight years old. He wore a Confederate hat, blunt, star-roweled spurs, and a set of .44 caliber Colts. By now he was known from the Rio Grande to the ranges of Montana.

Another of the Kid's sayings: "You learn things in the Army. You learn when a man's your commander, you say, 'yes, seh,' and do it."

Let's take a look at the Kid's ability with a gun: As he spoke Addis went for his gun. He drew with a high lift of his shoulders. It made his hands and arms too tense. He tried to reach too fast, grab too fast, shoot too fast. Pecos drew one gun. He drew with a hitch, a swing of his body, a pull of the trigger, all as careless as striking a match on the side of his pants. His bullet hit Addis and knocked him spinning. Pecos should have felt triumphant. He didn't. He just felt tired. He wished he could wash the sweat and powdersmoke off his hands and face.

Here is one more example: Rasmussen was still leaning over. The cup was in his left hand. In straightening, his right hand suddenly swung for

the six-shooter that rode low in a holster on his thigh. He'd telegraphed it with his eyes and Pecos, faster by a fifth of a second anyway, had him hopelessly beaten. Pecos drew with a backward dragging slap of his hand. He hesitated for a fragment of time. Then the gun came to life, lashing flame and lead across the room.

The Pecos Kid rode the trails with two sidekicks. One was HERNANDEZ FLANNIGAN. His real name was Pedro Gonzales y Fuento Jesus Maria Flannigan. His nickname was Butch. An Irish-Spanish halfbreed, he could imitate his father's brogue perfectly. He grew up in Chihuahua, spoke Spanish and English and Apache. He had mastered the 'deft' border-cross-draw and was naturally a first rate pistol man. He carried a bowie knife along with a guitar. The guitar he kept wrapped in a slicker right behind his saddle. He would make love to any woman at the drop of a hat. "Love to a Spaniard is no joke," he remarked. "Love is in the air he breathes and the wine he drinks." He was a handsome, debonaire man, with wavy black hair, flashing white teeth, a dark mustache, and moccasin-brown skin. He once told the Pecos Kid: "The coat of arms of my family, senor, ees one bullet hole rampant on the upside down sombrero." And his motto: "Shoot first and talk afterwards." His father was an Irish dragoon, a deserter, who ended up in Mexico. Hernandez also had an uncle who had been decorated by Santa Ana.

The second man was BIG JIM SWING, age twenty-five, with pale eyes and a mass of dunlap-colored hair, two hundred pounds of moving dynamite. He had a careless way about him that tended to minimize his frame and muscles, which were on the scale of a percheron horse. He was also the person designated to carry the accumulated funds of the trio, hidden somewhere on his body. Nobody, not even The Pecos Kid, tried to take that money away from him. They always asked first. Big Jim Swing wasn't the usual bundle of dumb muscle just hanging around. Here is an example: "The man was helpless in Big Jim's tremendous grip. Then, with a quickness unsuspected in one of his bulk, Jim shifted his hold, lifted the man and slammed him belly down across his bent knee. He let the man fall, writhing and helpless, to the ground."

This was another Thrilling publication and it seemd to have a lot going for it. According to pulpologist Albert Tonik there were some seventy-six novels from 1939 to 1953. As was the case with *Texas Rangers,* a variety of authors were involved, including Tom Curry (who originated the Rio Kid), C. William Harrison, Lee E. Wells, Dean Owen, Walker A. Tompkins, Gunnison Steele, Joseph Chadwick, D.B. Newton, Roe Richmond. Each one kept the stories moving at a fast clip Author John Dinan tells us again in his book, *The Pulp Western,* that "the fictional exploits of the Kid were interwoven with actual historical characters." These included the likes of Benito Juarez, Cochise, Geronimo, Gen. George Armstrong Custer, Wild Bill Hickok, Calamity Jane, Wyatt Earp, Pat Garrett, Judge Roy Bean—to list just a few.

It was my good fortune to secure (through the kindness of Al Tonik) several letters exchanged between author Tom Curry and Leo Margulies, the Editorial Director of the magazine. For exampe, one letter dated in June of 1939, has the following: "We were very much pleased with the way you handled the first Rio Kid story. I honestly think it's one of the best novels you've turned out." In another Curry said: "These pulp magazines used a 45,000—50,000 word (at times reduced to 30,000) novel with a series hero. It was necessary for the writer to submit a detailed outline before proceeding. As a rule Leo Margulies, editor-in-chief at Standard Magazines, also Better Publications, used experienced writers he knew and could depend upon. Now and then he would accept a newcomer." Incidentally, for the first and second novels, Curry received the sum of two hundred and fifty dollars. All of the correspondence is fascinating to read.

CAPTAIN ROBERT PRYOR was a handsome young giant, his rugged face burned bronze by the sun and wind of western out–trails. His eyes were blue, hair chestnut, cropped short, shoulders broad, tapered to the waist. He had a powerful chest. He wore blue breeches with the cavalry yellow stripe down the seam, tucked into expensive boots with Army spurs. He wore a blue shirt. His lean waist was strapped tight by a three-inch wide black leathere sword belt. Across his breast, two cartridge belts bearing leather holsters in which rode twin Colt .45's. Two more pistols were hidden in shoulder holsters under his clothing.

The Rio Kid was a man who had matured, but he had not killed his youth nor his humor. He was a man who made friends with Death. His habitual expectation in life was to be close to death, so he did not fear it. We have this report from a very early story: The line of Pryor's bronzed chin was set firm. His blue eyes were earnest, shot with a devil-may-care courage. The wide Stetson he wore to shield his eyes from the brilliant sun was cocked over his crisp, chestnut hair. Broad at the shoulders, his body tapered to narrow hips, and his was the ideal weight for a cavalryman. Across his chest were two cartridge belts, one to support a brace of pistols visible in holsters, and two hidden revolvers, sheathed under his armpits. His guns, with which he had grown expert from childhood and during the Civil War, gleamed in the sunlight. His leather was oiled and in good repair. A single glance at him showed power, the strength of a leader of men.

Pryor rode a mouse-colored dun named "Saber." This was "the breed that never dies," and "who loved the acrid smell of gunpowder." The horse was bony, long of leg, with no distinguishing marks except a black stripe down his back. Saber was not a sweet-tempered animal; he was given to biting and lashing out at strangers. "Only with his master did the dun reveal that he was something better than a wild, wicked mustang." The horse liked to hear Pryor hum an Army song: "Said the little black charger to the little white mare; The sergeant claims yore feed bill ain't really fair." Whenever the dun sensed trouble he would give his master warning that strangers were close at hand—a ripple of the black stripe down his back. Gen. George A. Custer said of the horse: "That dun of yours is a rascal, Captain. Always was. However, he's the fastest thing on four legs I've ever seen."

During the war Pryor had been wounded in the left side by a bullet. As a result, "the nerve over his rib cage itched when some innate warning contracted the skin." He also had one habit which he usually tried to perform each morning. It was a ritual practice with his revolvers: Draw and trigger, draw and trigger, faster and faster—until the movements were a blur. Having previously emptied his guns of bullets, they made no sound—a wise precaution in a very hostile land.

Here is a glimpse of Pryor taken from "The Rio Kid Rides Again," June of 1940: His blue eyes held a reckless, devil-may-care light that revealed something of his unfailing courage and power, He carried two fine, brown-steel Army Colts in a black-leather holster belt, and under his clothing two more small guns. His years as an Army man had given the Kid a military bearing, an air of command that nothing could eradicate. He had a passion for neatness, and his gear was always kept in meticulous order.

When Pryor returned to the Rio Grande country after his cavalry discharge, his destination was the family ranch. He remembered that below the house was a ford, "the best crossing for a hundred miles." As he neared the house he noted two graveled mounds.

When the homestead came into view he saw two men in the shade of the porch. "Four bits to cross," one man said. "I'm not crossing the river," Pryor replied. "Then git!" the man snapped. "We don't allow strangers here." Pryor looked at him. "What are you doing here? This is the Pryor ranch." The other man stared back. "Belongs to us these days." Then in just a few moments the Rio Kid's homecoming came in the form of gunsmoke. Hands went for their weapons. Seconds later two men were dead. The Rio Kid knew then that the two mounds were the graves of his parents.

Naturally there was a girl. Her name: Sally Brant. When Pryor had ridden off to the war, Sally was in her teens, a slim girl with golden curls down her back. By the time things got all sorted out the Rio Kid couldn't settle down to life on a cattle ranch. Like his sidekick said: "General, how could we ride together if you were married?' The Kid just laughed. "No danger yet," he said.

Pryor's "sidekick" was a young Mexican named CELESTINO MIRELES. Pryor once saved his life from the hands of some rather nasty Rio Grande outlaws. Mireles wore the costume of his native land south of the border: A gold-braided charro jacket, flare-bottomed gaucho pants, a bell-tasseled sombrero with a steeple-peaked crown, high-heeled Hermosillo boots fitted with star-roweled Spanish spurs. HIs father, Vincente Mireles, was a big Mexican land owner. His hacienda was large, his cattle herd vast. Celestino's father, and now the son alike, had blue-black straight hair and black eyes, a curved nose over a strong but beautiful mouth. Celestino Mireles had a deep respect for his parents. He was an excellent rider, having been able to "stay on a horse's back before he could toddle."

Celestino swore allegiance to the Rio Kid, ready to follow him anywhere (which is exactly what he did). The Kid saw that the lad could not be budged from his purpose. Celestino had a keen mind, with far above average intelligence, and had been carefully schooled by tutors in riding, cattle raising, hunting, trailing. Like all Mexican he "loved the long knife and was adept at using it." He usually called Pryor "My General."

Here is a segment from the second novel, "The Trail Blazers," Winter 1940:

"The carpetbaggers got our state in their grip and the iron heel has ground us down," Colonel White said. "Yuh look like a soldier yore-ownself. Would it be too presumin' if I asked did yuh ride for Jeb Stuart? Yun got all the earmarks of a good cavalryman."

All eyes fixed on the Rio Kid, squatted in the center of the circle. "I was a cavalryman, Colonel," he replied, his voice gentle, "but not for Jeb Stuart, who was one of the best. I rode for General Custer." A stunned silence fell on them. Women's eyes grew frightened, and several of the men dropped their hands towards their pistols. "A traitor!" a hot-headed ex-officer growled. "He fought for the damn Yankees!"

The Rio Kid challenged with unblinking stare. "Why, sah, that's where yuh're wrong," he said calmly. "Every man fought in the war as his inside self told him. Mine said stay with the Union. Now the war's over and done with, though, and there's no need for folks to be enemies no more."

The stately Colonel White rose to his feet and balanced himself on his wooden leg. "This gentlemen," he said courteously, "is our guest. There's sense in what he says, though a man may think as he likes."

Pryor was orry for these people, his own kind. He knew bitterness was in their hearts. He wished to help them, and pondered a way.

The Rio Kid was one of the few characters we did a Chronological Study on. We thought the reader might be interested:

YEAR	AGE	EVENT
1843		Born—Rio Grande country of Texas. Nearest town identified as Brewster.
1844	1	Joseph Smith, founder of the Mormons, killed in Carthage.
1845	2	Texas admitted to the Union—December 29th.
1846	3	Mormons settle in Salt Lake City under Brigham Young.
1852	9	*Uncle Tom's Cabin* written by Harriet Beecher Stowe.
1856	13	Abolitionist John Brown organized anti-slavery group at Ossowatomie, Kansas.
1858	15	Lincoln-Douglas debates.
1860	17	Lincoln elected President.
1861	18	CIVIL WAR: Robert Pryor joins the Union forces, feeling that loyalty to country was greater than to the state. He spent all four years in the cavalry. First assignment was probably with 1st Platoon, G Company, Second Cavalry, where he met Second Lieutenant George A. Custer. We believe he also saw duty with the 5th Cavalry. Pryor would often recall later a remark Custer once made: "When your enemy is stronger than you, maneuver your forces so that enemy gets a little of what he wants and at the same time you get a little of what you want."

At one time or another, Pryor served under the following in the capacity of an aide or scout: Gen. Custer, Gen. Philip Sheridan (then Commander, Army of the Potomac), Gen. William Sherman, Gen. George C. Meade, Gen. Granville Dodge (Commander, 16th Army Corps during the campaign for Atlanta), Gen. U.S. Grant, who on March 12, 1864 was named General-in-Chief, Armies of the Potomac, by President Lincoln. Pryor also performed a service for President Lincoln during the war. Numerous missions were carried out in '63 for various other high-ranking officers.

On 2 October 1862, President Lincoln met with Gen. George C. McClellan. We believe Pryor was present because of his association with the high-level commanders. Pryor rose quickly in rank and by war's end held the brevet rank of captain. (This simply means it was a commission giving an officer a higher rank than that for which he received pay.) His captain's commission was signed by President Lincoln. (Later on Pryor would carry credentials signed by President Grant.)

Pryor would also have served in the 3rd Division, U.S. Cavalry Corps. His battles included: Bull Run, Antietam, Gettysburg, Shiloh. He definitely came up against Major J.E.B. Stuart's cavalry. It is a known fact that Pryor's life was saved just before Vicksburg by a man named Brannon. Pryor had somehow been caught by some Confederate cavalry. He was wounded, although not very seriously, during the battle of Gettysburg. The result was a scar on his side. The flesh healed unevenly, and whenever danger threatened, the cicatrized section reacted differently from surrounding tissue and would begin to twitch. This would serve as a barometer, warning him of danger and even of weather changes. (Pryor also knew how to treat wounds.)

During the Battle of Atlanta, Pryor served as an aide to Gen. Sherman. He witnessed the burning on 2 September, 1864. Another established fact was that Pryor was present on 19 November, 1863, when President Lincoln gave his address at Gettysburg.

April 9, 1865, Lee surrendered to Grant at Appomattox Court House. Pryor was there in his capacity as Custer's aide-de-camp. For the ceremony Grant wore a private's blouse with the three stars of his rank. There were eight other Union officers in the room. At Grant's side was Maj. Gen. Philip Sheridan. Custer stood in the far corner, directly behind Col. Elys Parker.

Shortly afterwards Pryor was on orders for cavalry duty in Washington, D.C. On 14 April President Lincoln was shot in Ford's Theater by actor John Wilkes Booth. Pryor was ordered, along with other cavalrymen, to scout the countryside for the assassin. Twelve days later found Pryor among those who were present at a barn near Bowling Green, Virginia, where Booth had concealed himself. The man who shot Booth at that time was identified as Boston Corbett, a Union soldier.

Pryor was mustered out some time in May, 1865. He headed straight for Texas.

| 1865 | 23 | Pryor found Texas under the heel of Yankee carpetbaggers, returning Unionists, and renegades. A man known as The Eagle, with his marauding band, had killed his parents and taken over the homestead. The town of Brewster was under The Eagle's domination. At the same time General Sherman was placed in charge of Texas and the Mexican border district, directly under Gen. Sheridan. Gen. Custer was picked to help clean things up. In time, the Eagle was brought to justice and peace was restored. The Rio Kid then "took leave of the people he had restored to their birthright and headed west in search of adventure." |

1868 25

The year was so identified twice in one novel in regard to the Washita and Custer: (1) "Besides, the soldiers will hunt for us if we strike. Pahuska—Long Hair—whom you call Custer, defeated the Indians on the Washita." (2) Custer had just brought his regiment back from the Washita when a long struggle against the Indians had proved successful. (Note: November 27, 1868, Custer's cavalry attacked the winter camp of Black Kettle's Cheyenne. It was a massacre.)

Custer and Pryor met along the Chisum Trail. After the war Custer had come to Texas where "he demonstrated against the invaders of Mexico and at the same time assisted the Rio Kid in smashing a clique of carpetbaggers preying on the Kid's homeland." (This marked the second meeting between Pryor and Custer in the postwar years.)

1869 26

The Rio Kid and Celestino Mireles headed eastward on the Texas Trail into the Buffalo Country of Kansas. Pryor had been offered a job as a marshal by Wild Bill Hickok. But it seemed that Hickok had gotten into a scrape in Hays, Kansas, with three of Custer's troopers. Hickok killed them and ran. His destination was Ellsworth, Kansas. 1869 was the year Hickok did have trouble in Hays.

Note: Depicted in the third story is the Battle of Adobe Walls. The attack force was led by Chief Quannah Parker. He was backed by hundreds of Comanche and allied braves. Adobe Walls was a post in the Panhandle of Texas. Among the white men present was Bat Masterson. (However, the battle did not actually occur until June 27, 1874, which puts it out of sequence in relation to Bob Pryor's adventures. [Let's simply call this 'author's prerogative.' It's the same kind of thing pulpologist Albert Tonik ran into while researching the background of Texas Ranger Jim Hatfield.]

But by no means allow this glitch to turn you away from the Rio Kid. The stories are great!)

Rio Kid

Sally Brant

Celestino Mireles

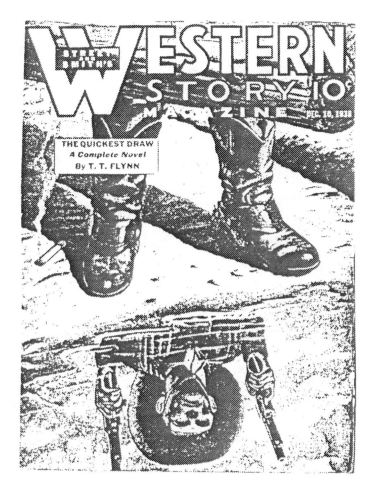

THE SHOOTING GALLERY KID

The above-named magazine featured a very unlikely candidate for the role in which he was depicted. Known as The Shooting Gallery Kid, he can be found in the August 7, 1943 and October 30, 1943 issues. The author, Ryerson Johnson, who had these comments: "The Shooting Gallery Kid came along when the western pulps were winding down fast. *Western Story* had dropped their basic rate from two cents to one and a half. We were really seeing the writing on the wall. I was moving out into the mystery field. The westerns were disappearing fast, out of the pulps into the television tube."

The author had first submitted the stories to Popular Publications, but they put thumbs down, so he had to look elsewhere.

The Shooting Gallery Kid was named WAH LEE. He was fat, good-natured, Americanized, though retaining the overall wisdom and pbnilosophy of the East. He was young, pleasant looking, with a face that was somehow sad. He weighed around two hundred pounds and said things like: "It is written by Chinese, wise men don't count chickens outside of cooking pot."

Wah Lee claimed to have attained his ability and dexterity with frontier hardware in a San Francisco shooting gallery. That means he usually carried a gun, but there was definitely something else: "He flipped very small and very deadly sharp-pointed weapons," Johnson told me. "These were thin-fingered knives from China, and within a limited range just as deadly as bullets." Wah Lee carried them inside a carpet bag. When ready for use they were concealed inside his coat, an even dozen, six to a side, inserted in loop sheathes. The coat itself was big enough to have "wrapped around a big elephant."

Here is a description; the scene is the Pick and Shovel Saloon: "The man standing in front of me patiently across the bar is Chinese. He is wearing a black broadcloth coat, and it hangs on him so loose that even though it's a coat, it looks

like a kimono. There is a kind of flashing in my eyes, and I draw in my stomach, and the flashing flashes past me, and then I hear a tiny ping. I keep on moving, like a nightmare, but not believing my senses. I move right on past Idaho Jug and he doesn't even inch his gun from the holster. There was a thin-bladed knife pinning Idaho Jug's coat sleeve to the wall, thereby for the moment anchoring his six gun to its holster. Someone in the room had tossed that knife, slicing it past me to set Idaho Jug's sleeve."

Here is another: "Then suddenly, out of nowhere, a flame came lancing. That was what it seemed like at first glance, a glinting in the yellow lamplight. The knife pierced Haime's upraised hand with a small thud. So fast it was almost ludicrous, Haime's gun-raised hand had stilled, almost as though it was nailed to the wall. He stared at the knife when he pulled it free. It was a peculiar instrument, thin and long and delicate as a surgeon's blade, the

handle filigreed brass inset with cinnabar."

Then another hombre made the mistake of going for his gun: "There was another of those nasty sounding little thuds. Dick Yellin, in a panic, tugged at his holstered gun. He just tugged, that was all. Alarmingly, the gun didn't slide from leather. He looked down. The holster was pinned tightly closed by another of those sinister knives with the blade thinner than a man's finger, and a handle brass-weighted for perfect balance and throwing."

For sure those knives could be just about as deadly as bullets. We remarked earlier that Wah Lee carried a gun. The following scene tells us about that: I happened to be watching the Chinese boy, and I guess I never saw a fat man move so fast. The hand gripping the chunky arm as though to hold the blood in, came away, and with it, appearing there like magic, was a thin, mean-looking target pistol. The Kid shoved the pistol against Crummy Patterson's stomach. "So solly inconvenience causing," he said, " but tell everybody drop gun fast or regretfully put bullet through you."

Wah Lee rode the trail with two other gents, DOUBLE-TROUBLE DAWSON and MOUSE HAGGERTY. First off, Dawson was a big blond, handsome, hell-for-leather cowpoke with his heart on his sleeve and his brains in his holster. He was an extrovert. Mouse was an introverted, quiet, mild little man, but very smart. He was the trio's brains. He really didn't go for violence at all. His favorite weapon, a cow's tail filled at one end with sand and sewed tight shut. He swung the thing like a blackjack. The two of them viewed Wah Lee like this: "Young, fat, bland, sleepy-eyed, looking as innocent as a cupid on a valentine." But men trying to take advantage of him had found him to be as deadly as a nest of sidewinders in a dark camp.

the
SILVER KID

Real Western, published every other month by Columbia Publications, Inc., Robert W. Lowndes, editor. Cost, 15 cents. It featured a character known as The Silver Kid, real name Solo Strant. He wore a black, double-fronted shirt with a twin row of silver buttons, black batwing chaps with silver conches at the flaps, double gunbelts with the guns rigged butts foward for the deadly cross-arm draw. The butts were of silver. He wore spurs fashioned from Mexican silver dollars. On his head was a weather–warped black sombrero with a sil-ver-decorated band. On the chin strap of the sombrero, at his throat, he wore a little silver skull.

Here is a segment from "Shadow of the Sil-ver Kid," as written by T. W. Ford: The Kid's fingers went to that silver skull at his throat as he grew more and more impatient. Then the Kid's right hand was sliding across his body in the cross-draw even before he swung towards the front door. Three men were coming in fast, guns out and ready. A fourth one in a red shirt was just behind them. One gun breathed muzzle flame twice; slugs chunked into the bar front. But the Kid wasn't in that spot; he'd slid sideward and the gun in his right hand an-swered. Shots rattled from it. The red-shirted one in the doorway who'd fired first jumped back outside, cursing, nicked in the shoulder. The other two had jumped back outside and fanned out. A bullet nicked the Kid's hat brim. Backed to the rear of the bar in the corner, the Kid wheeled to his left. He sighted the man outside the window across the room, shooting from the alley. The Kid triggered twice. His first slug missed. The Kid's second bullet caught the back of the gunman's hand. The fingers splayed out in sudden pain. The gent's smoking weapon thudded to the floor inside. The hand with the red band of flowing blood on it was jerked from sight. But the drygul-cher bore the Kid's bullet brand, the track of a glug on his gun hand. And that sign inevitably spelled early death for those who bore it.

Solo Strant rode a paint horse. He also had a brother by the name of Hondo. The brother was an expert when it came to using a knife. Hondo was almost the image of his brother, and maybe just a tiny bit taller than the Kid himself. He had the same wasp waist, the al-most fragile look, the same black hair with a loose lock hanging at one side of the forehead of his lean V-shaped face. But the eyes alone were different, being round and lighter than the Kid's dark sleepy-looking ones. Solo had thought the brother had been killed in a fire when he was only a child, four years of age. That same blaze gutted most of the small cowtown where he'd been born. It also killed his father and mother, burned to death in their small cabin. Solo at the time was seven years of age. Following the burial of the three pine coffins in boot hill, Solo's Uncle John had taken him to his own home, several hundred miles away across a state line. Although the brother went by the name of Hondo, he had been christened Jeff Strant. His mother's name was Beryl; his father's was Fred. In their early years together, the two brothers had a puppy named Maverick.

PAT STEVENS, SAM SLOAN, and ONE-EYED EZRA.

Real Western also featured another of those three-men combinations much like The Range Riders. But these three were just a little bit different. Their names were PAT STEVENS, SAM SLOAN, and ONE-EYED EZRA.

First of all, Stevens was Sheriff of Powder Valley, "a man more at home on a horse than in a swivel chair." His office was located in the Court House of Dutch Springs. Tall, lean of hip, with gray eyes, he rode a sorrel horse.

The second member, Sam Sloan, was short, thick across the shoulders, eyes deep-set above a crooked nose. "A blunt stubble of beard prickled his aggressive chin." Usually his attire consisted of a "greasy stained hickory shirt and greasy pants."

The third man, One-Eyed Ezra, was big, red-headed. One eye was closed, lid lying flat. "The wound that had taken the eyes showed features slanting up diagonally across the eyelid and over the temple into the hair. When he sat on his horse he resembled a shaggy bear. He had a deep voice. Neither Ezra nor Sloan were considered to be paragons of beauty, but Pat Stevens could say that better men never sided a partner.

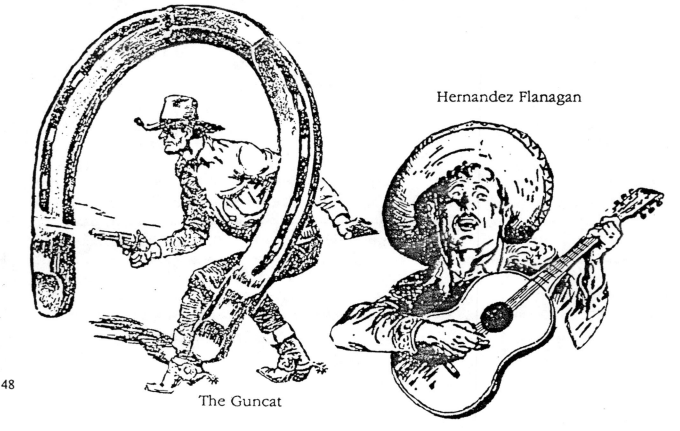

Hernandez Flanagan

The Guncat

48

BERT LITTLE

The magazine: *Western Trails* (Two-Gun Stories of the Real West). It was published monthly by Magazine Publishers, Inc., costing 15 cents. Many a well-known author wrote for it, including the likes of Joe Archibald, Lester Dent, Frank Gruber, Charles Marquis Warren, Frederick C. Davis. (The Duke Buckland series came from the Davis typewriter.) Buckland was a hombre with cold blue eyes and was very handy with a Colt. Joe Archibald penned the adventures of WALRUS McGONNIGLE and WISHBONE WATTERS, "two mavericks of the wasteland."

But one of the individuals who rode the dusty western trails answered to the name of BERT LITTLE. The author: Clyde A. Warden. The stories read well and flow with steady action. The hero "was lightning fast with his guns as well as his bone-crushing fists." (On one of the covers he was depicted as looking quite a lot like Tom Mix).

Little was a silent, grim sort of man, who once said: "A dead hero is a poor kind of hero." He did have a pretty common name, but don't let that fool you. He once warned a hombre this way: "I'm asking you to pick your words more carefully when you're speaking to me. I don't like the sound of them." He stood there at the bar and watched, his smile turning to a mask of grimness. The cold, bright gleam in his gray eyes smouldered deeper. "I'm pretty much the kind that likes to be left alone." He paused for a moment. "A man can only die once and after it's over with, he's got nothin' left to bother about."

Little was a tall, lean, broad-shouldered man, with muscles of pure steel. Weight, 190 pounds. He was a strikingly handsome person, strong-jawed, square-chinned. Face, sun-bronzed, lean. His smile was a different sort of smile than most others. It was that of a man who rides a trail of danger which has no end to it—a faint smile, lonely, somehow grim and somehow gentle. Eyes, cold, calm, stern, cool. Color, blue-gray, with a pale, bright flame gleaming in their depths. To put it another way, they were like ice, deep, clear, almost blinding like the rays of the sun. They often did gleam with a white fire such as the sun makes in reflecting from the surface of new steel. Death lurked in their depths and mounted slowly to the surface when he became angry. He had a way of holding up his head that spoke eloquently of undying courage. His voice was rich, low, gentle, yet with a steel-like ring to it. His ears seemed to be tuned to wilderness voices. He could have heard the falling of a leaf in a moss-carpeted forest, or the noiseless padded feet of a panther stalking its prey, or could have followed the song of a tiny bird perched high in the top of a tree from beginning to end.

Strength just seemed to radiate from Bert Little. About him there was no hint of fear, only a mighty calm and a grim steadiness in his manner. He said very little, but remarked: "Down along the border the men don't do a lot of talking. They're pretty busy most of the time, seeking that they keep alive."

Little was like a cat. He had the litheness and the swift, sure balance of a cat. Once he fell downwards a dozen feet or more, a fall that would have broken the neck of almost any other man. He twisted over, whirling in mid-air, so that he landed on his feet. His body was a mass of scars from bullets and knife cuts. His one habit was that he smoked roll-your-own cigarettes. He was not averse to taking a drink. When he stood up, he gained his feet with an easy flowing movement. His handshake was strong, firm. He had a strange outlook that went: "I'm a stranger hereabouts. I belong to nobody but myself. A man is what he makes of himself, not what he's branded."

A stranger once told Little: "You're a strange man. You are not like a Spaniard. You are not like an American. You are like no one but Bert Little. You have learned to live your life the way it was put before you. You are a young man but have learned to be yourself. You have the courage and strength of a giant. You have a mind and heart that is clean. You have become what few men in all time have equalled, a great fighter."

Still others along the Rio Grande spoke of his smile: "They saw the smile change. They saw it go to the corners of his lips and twist the corners into hard, grim lines of recklessness."

When Little rode into some border town, he sat erect in the saddle, head high, face straight before him. But out of the tail of his eyes he had searched the dark face of each building. It was a natural action, a habit formed through long trails of danger. Little had also learned the art of moving silently. He was a master at this. At times he seemed almost supernatural. So whether it was a gun or a knife, it mattered not to Bert Little: "There was a long, slender icicle of a knife gripped in the man's hand. With a chopping stroke of his hand, Little laid the iron-hand edge of his palm across the man's wrist. The knife fell away."

Here is just a short segment as Little is about to step into action: "A breathless silence had fallen upon the room. None of them there in the cantina doubted the fact that death was near and that it would suddenly, in all its ghastly form, make itself known."

Unlike most, Little had no human sidekicks. Instead there were his horse KING and his dog BUCK. The two were often pictured as follows: "The horse ran without effort, floating along with the speed and ease of a bird on the wing. And beside him, with a long and tireless lope, ran Buck."

King had once roamed free as the leader of a band of wild horses. He could walk with the silence of a stalking cat when necessary. The horse was a golden red, deep-chested stallion that always seemed to move effortlessly. His stride was as smooth as the drifting sweep of the wind. His mane like silver. His muscles were of pure steel, riffling like the flowing currents of a river.

Buck looked like a wolf, but he was leaner and bigger and far more dangerous. He had a great muscled body, big, uplifting head, gleaming white fangs. When the dog sensed danger the hair of its neck would bristle as he growled softly, long white fangs bared. Buck commanded almost as much respect as Little himself. It took only a touch of his master's hand to flatten the dog on the ground. And after that signal the great dog would not stir or utter a sound even if an unseen person should step directly on him. Buck also reacted to hand signals. "Buck and King," Little had said, "they're not just a horse and a dog. They're my friends."

Bert Little was a man who could handle guns with great dexterity. It was really nothing short of amazing. He wore twin Colts, both especially built so they balanced in the hand to a hair's breadth of weight. The butts were of burnt ivory with the head of a longhorn steer carved on the side. He sometimes wore guns beneath his armpits with spring holsters. This change of position never lessened his speed when he had to draw, for he practiced long hours in drawing from both hips and shoulders. Here are two examples: (1) No one saw him draw. His guns leaped into his hands like magic. The room filled with the roar of weapons and the flash of flame.

(2) The hands of Little became a blur of brown at his side. It seemed that one of his ivory-handled guns actually appeared out of thin air before him. The polished steel of its long barrel flashed brightly in the firelight. He stood motionless as a great oak tree and in his hand, the ivory-handled Colt was leaping as it sang its thunderous song.

Here is a dramatic event that took place in a saloon: Little raised his hands and reached across the bar. Iron fingers closed upon the half-breed's throat. Then the man was lifted up and over the bar to Little's side. He just held him there, choking, bent far backwards acorss his knees. He loosened his grip. "You're only half an inch from hell," spoke Little. "You better spend your time talkin' or that time is gonna be cut mighty short."

Naturally Little met quite a few women along the way. We'll describe just one of them; her name was Lee Maple: She was straight and slender as a willow. Perhaps her shoulders were just a trifle wide. But even so, they added to the feeling of strength about her. She had perfect poise and sureness. One could see the power in her blue eyes, in the set firmness of her curved red lips; in every feature of her golden-bronzed face. Her hair was like burnished gold.

Little encountered some pretty dastardly villains. Here are some of them: THE UNSEEN ONE, who summoned Little to an ancient ghost town; THE RED RAIDERS, a marauding killer band along the border brakes; SENOR DEATH, a masked rider of mystery; THE HEADLESS ONE—a headless thing of white light; THE RATTLER, whose true identity was always kept concealed behind a snake-skin mask; THE BLACK SHADOW, a hombre who simply would not die.

One of the villains who faced Little looked like this: He was big and broad of shoulder. He stepped with the ease and grace that a huge cat steps. His face was an olive bronze, as set and hard as if carved in stone. His black eyes gleamed like the smooth, bright surface of ice. Upon his cheek was a scar that pulled his thin lips into a perpetual sneer. There was everything about the man that was evil, even to the long and slender fingers of his hands. He carried his weapons in a way that proved he knew how to use them: upon either thigh, low slung and snugly tied, was a scarred and well-worn holster. From them protruding high and free were the butts of a pair of finely kept revolvers. At his belt was a sheath knife, its pearl handle shining brightly against his black shirt. He also carried a whip.

Pulp collector Lester Belcher said this about Little: "He's a strange man, and one that just stays in your memory."

Robert Sampson, writing in his article "A Time of Lively Fiction," made the following remarks that became relevant not only to the western hero like Bert Little, but all pulp heroes at large: "These men are free. These men achieve splendidly. They resolve their fictional problems in a way that makes mere reality pallid and plain. Their blazing guns are never exhibits at a murder trial. Nor are these men corrupted by power. Their judgments are correct; their actions justified." Amen!

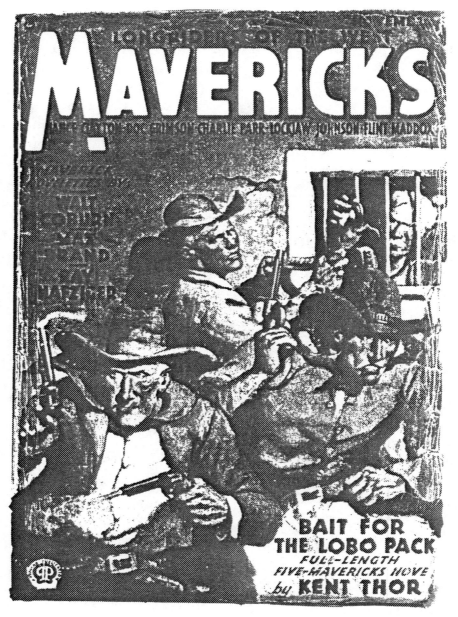

A Popular Publication. The author: Ken Thorne. Cost: 15 cents and worth it. The word is action from start to finish. There were five individuals involved, all of them inseparable knights of the saddle—the LONG RIDERS OF THE WEST. The "Mavericks" were bound together by the immortal bonds of outlaw friendship. There were few places between the Canadian border and Mexico City that didn't talk of the Five Mavericks and their gunsmoke exploits. They were outlaws of a very special brand. None of the five had ever killed a man, except in open warfare. Whenever they carried through a robbery or loaned their guns to the side of the underdog in any range trouble, the affair went off without injury to ordinary citizens. Let me introduce you to them:

<u>CHARLIE PARR</u>

He, along with one other, headed the fearless gunhawks. He was an old timer on the trails, with a weather-tanned face, white mustache, blue eyes that were set in a mass of wrinkles. He had a wiry, spidery figure. He had been a member of the notorious Boothill Kennedy Gang at one time.

MAVERICKS

LOCKJAW JOHNSON

He had a long, horse-like face and was known for his great loyalty. A man who asked no questions and had no reservations. He had known Parr and went with him after leaving the Kennedy bunch.

FLINT MADDOX

Hard-fisted, melancholy-eyed. Former rancher who had been ruined by a neighboring land-hog. Wife and children had all died in a fire. As a result, he shot the ranchman and his foreman in a saloon duel, then was forced outside the law by a crooked sheriff.

LANCE CLAYTON

Young, big-shouldered, buoyant. A man of 190 pounds of steel-hard bone and muscle. It seemed he encountered the "Longriders of the West" by reason of a faithless lady who was in some financial trouble. He held up a saloon in her interest, turned all the money taken in the robbery over to her, then left just a single jump ahead of a posse.

DOC GRIMSON

He also headed the Mavericks. He was a gambler, his past hidden, unknown. He had lumi-nous gray eyes and "his gun hand moved with the lightning, flickering speed of a rattlesnake's tongue." It seemed, moreover, he had a reputation of "complete fearlessness," and was deadly with his guns. He would stick with a friend right up to hell's gate and back again.

COVERS BELOW BY ROBERT G. HARRIS

SEÑOR RED MASK

The character: SEÑOR RED MASK. The author: Guy L. Maynard. His real name was TOM GOODWIN, owner of the Bar G Ranch. His father, a member of the Protective Association, was killed during a raid on the ranch. In the disguise of Senor Red Mask, often called simply "Red Mask," he was a fascinating character in his own right. He wore a black velvet silver-trimmed charro costume, a scarlet silk mask, silver-laced black sombrero with a very high crown, twin Colts with pearl stocks holstered beneath a gray silk sash that encircled his waist. His spurs were of silver. "I am Senor Red Mask, a rider of justice and killer of devils!" he echoed as he sat astride a black stallion called Thunder. He had a rich tenor voice. He was another individual who habitually talked to his horse: The weird hoot of an owl broke the stillness of the moonlit Mexican night. Tom Goodwin listened for the answering call. It came—faint, muted by distance, from far down the trail that led southward across the Chihuahua rangeland. "Those birds are right musical tonight, Thunder," Senor Red Mask muttered into the flagged ears of his mount. "I wonder now, if it don't mean there's trouble brewing on the border."

Here is a scene from "Lobo Brand for a Caballero," October 17, 1942 issue:

"You cannot pass, senor," the guard said.

"You couldn't stop me," Senor Red Mask declared. His right hand rose in a chopping motion. The guard's protest was ended abruptly. He dropped without a sound.

Whenever anyone went down under his flaming guns, particularly somebody wanted by the law, Senor Red Mask left his insignia: "A stunted sagebrush grew close at hand. He plucked two green sprigs of the fragrant plant. Bending over the body, he placed the two bits of sage on the man's chest. It was the "bad-man brand" of old border days—now the mark of Senor Red Mask.

From a story titled "Gunrunner's Brand," we are treated to a view of his gun prowess: The right hand of Senor Red Mask twitched in a blurred streak too fast for the eye to follow. A silver coin spun high in the air, glinting in the sunlight. As it reached the peak of its upward flight, a six-gun blasted in the caballero's hand. The coin abruptly disappeared. A wintery smile quirked the spike points of Senor Red Mask's jaunty little dark mustache. "You will find the dobe peso in the chaparral, hombre," he murmured in a voice soft as fur on a cougar's claws, and with the same menace. "And I am waiting for you to shoot me. Proceed, senor."

But Bill Hooker was staring in pop-eyed amazement and fear. Such marksmanship as he had just witnessed was uncanny! The hand gripping his six-gun jerked away as though the stock had suddenly scorched his fingers. Senor Red Mask slid his smoke-dribbling Colt into its silver-riveted holster under his sash.

Tom Goodwin's favorite song was "La Paloma." While in the guise of Senor Red Mask he very often lighted up a cigarro. But many who followed his adventures will most likely always recall him like this: He pulled up his snorting black, coolly reloaded his smoking Colts while he watched with eyes that glinted like cracked ice through the holes in his scarlet mask.

He also had another personality known as El Muchacho, a poor peon youth who played a battered guitar and sang catchy Mexican songs. He wore cheap cotton garments, a huge sombrero of palm fibers, dark-sole-leather guarachas on his feet. Over his broad shoulders lay a gaudy serape. He rode a buckskin pony.

He was given assistance by a "faithful Mexican-Indian of middle age known as Gray Eagle. The Indian was a powerfully built man, with a dignified bearing about him." He rode a leggy roan horse. Gray Eagle once told Tom Goodwin, after hearing the howling of a coyote: "When the coyote howls like that, it means death will soon strike." Once when the sky overhead was streaked with red-and-yellow cloud effects, he remarked: "It is a war-painted sky. There will be a battle today.":

If Senor Red Mask was somehow involved, you can be sure it'd be a battle!

 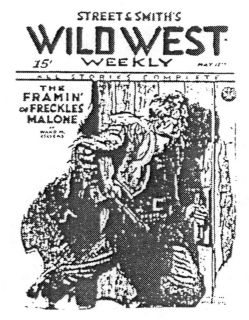

FRECKLES MALONE

The above-named magazine featured a character from the pen of Ward M. Stevens known as FRECKLES MALONE. (Stevens' real name was Paul S. Powers.) We only read seven or eight of the stories prior to typing this article, but then were fortunate to locate several more. Each one kept us on the edge of the chair, as the action moved ever so swiftly.

Freakles was a clean-cut young redhead. Hair, violently red, face spotted with freckles "from the roots of his flaming red hair down to the cleft in his square chin." Eyes were blue, keen, penetrating, "the steely glint that filtered down between his lashes had been put there by the frontier." He was slender of built except for powerful, compact and broad shoulders from which he radiated power down to the toes of his high-heeled, Spanish-spurred boots. Not an ounce of fat was revealed on his wiry, trim body. He moved with an easy grace that commanded respect.

Among those close to Malone was a young Swede, SWEN SWENSON, a big man, raw-boned, a first-class fighting fool and the best cook in all of Arizona Territory. He carried around a heavy .50 caliber Sharpes rifle be-cause he was simply a poor shot with a six-gun. People often misjudged this big fellow with a moon-like face topped by a thatch of yellow hair. His hands and feet seemed enormous, but in spite of his clumsiness he was exceedingly strong. His one pride and joy was in cooking flapjacks. He did make the best flapjacks Malone ever tasted in his entire life. "And when ay am cookin' flapyacks ay ben the boss!" Swenson bellowed.

At first Malone worked for one John Butter-field of the Butterfield Overland Mail Company, with headquarters in Tucson, Arizona. The year was 1858. The coaches carried both mail and passengers between St. Louis and San Francisco via the southern deserts. Relay stations were fifteen-sixteen miles apart. The U.S. Cavalry was often detailed to escort the coaches through Apache territory in Arizona and New Mexico. When Malone carried the mail he wore tight-fitting doeskin trousers, small high-heeled boots, a light flannel shirt laced at the front with buckskin thongs, and a Colt .45. (In time Malone became the young-est superintendent of the Southern Overland.) But finally Malone quit Butterfield. With

Swenson, he went to work for the Overland outfit of Russel, Majors, and Waddell—as a rider and as chief cook. Malone's pay was a hundred dollars. Later Malone was offered a job in a St. Louis bank for a much higher salary, which he promptly turned down. Malone's ability with a gun was demonstrated many times: "Once again his .45 roared into action. He was fighting mad, his red hair standing on end like the bristles of a porcupine, and his teeth were bared like a cornered cougar's."

His draw was bewilderingly fast: "A vivid flash of lavender, as sudden as summer heat lightning, came in a gust. A dull, booming report echoed off across the jagged rocks above. There was a horrible, rasping yell from the tall whiskered outlaw as a bullet clipped his throat. Dropping the gun, he fell to his knees in the thick smoke, strangling and coughing, a wave of crimson blotting out the blue of his flannel shirt."

Here now is another view of Freckles Malone as he prepares to carry the mail: "He vaulted into the saddle and turned the pinto's head westward. Out of the cholla canyon he sailed, leaving the silver-green of the cactus behind him as he climbed the vast floor of the mesa. On both sides the lava hills rose in weird formation, a blend of two colors in the sun. Tall giant cactus dotted the landscape, rising over the spears of the red-tipped ocotillo. In all the desert world nothing moved."

There was one thing Malone always kept reminding people that he met: "Will you please stop callin' me 'Mr. Malone'? Freckles is the name—just plain Freckles Malone. When anybody calls me 'Mr.' three times in a row, I generally get mad. Let that be a warnin'."

Once when Malone became trapped in some quicksand, the following incident took place:

Malone: "Throw me that rope." He held up his six-gun, a deadly glitter in his eyes.

Voice: "And what if I don't?" the other replied.

Malone: "I'll shoot to kill."

Voice: "Killin' me won't save yuh. Yuh'll die, too."

Malone: "But I'll have the satisfaction of takin' yuh with me, yuh rattlesnake. I'm givin' yuh until the count of three to throw me that rope. One—two—"

Voice: "Don't shoot. I—I was only foolin'. I'll pull yuh out."

Finally, one more glimpse of Freckles in action: "The big six-gun in Malone's hand suddenly changed from a lifeless piece of steel mechanism to a death-dealing thunderbolt. As the other guns opened up, the redhead's Colt spurted flame and smoke, a succession of stabbing crimson flashes that cut the gloom like fiery knives.

TENSLEEP MAXON

The above-named magazine was a Popular Publication, price ten cents. Over the years many writers contributed stories, including the likes of Walt Coburn, Ray Nafzinger, Harry F. Olmsted, and Bart Cassidy. Numerous covers were painted by Walter M. Baumhofer.

The character we are interested in was TENSLEEP MAXON. The author: Bart Cassidy. "He could be dangerous when crossed, but more likely to talk than shoot." At one time there was a thousand dollar reward on his head. Even when he was almost broke, Tensleep usually kept a half sawbuck in the sweatband of his hat for emergency. Along the way he rode a variety of horses with names like Piebald, Red Eye, and High Ball. This outlaw samaritan also called himself a "horse dealer." He knew horse flesh for sure and couldn't be fooled. He also went by a variety of names: Hardrock Jones, Catastrophe Jones, and in "Tensleep, Doctor of Gunsmoke," December 1935, he was Doc Pulmonary Jones: "Where's the Doc?" the man asked as he came into the office. "He's sick in bed. I'm sidin' him," Tensleep replied. "Git yore bag," he ordered, drawin' his brows. "I've got a sick friend. I want you should attend him." He whipped out a gun. Tensleep wondered just what to do. The answer came quickly as the man took his pistol.

The usual description of Tensleep Maxon was as follows: Age twenty-seven, five feet nine inches tall, weight around one hundred and thirty pounds, sandy complexion.

One thing had better be explained right fast. The stories were all written in the first person, which is "the nominative case of the pronoun of the first person, by which a person denotes himself." Anyhow, don't let that keep you from checking this hombre out. For instance, when it came to the game of poker, Tensleep remarked: "Poker will keep but trouble waits for no man. Draw yore bets an' don't git broiled in another man's wars. You've got plenty of yore own."

From "Tensleep Laws A Town," March 1938, we have this action view: "I am mad. An' the best shootin' I ever done, I done right there. I hit the trigger. My slug takes that old buzzard in the neck, killin' him in the saddle. He throws up his hands, lets out a squawk an' heaves overside. He falls free an' Red Eye swerves to the boardwalk like the nice little pony he is. Yeah, I rage, weep yore heads off for him. Say all the nice things yuh kin for a man that died fer you. But for gosh sake don't

do nothing tuh back up yore marshal. Marshals is cheap and yore precious hide is hard tuh patch up when bullet burnt. Stand here an' watch him shot down an' never lift a finger."

In "Meet Sheriff Tensleep," May 1938, after they got things all cleaned up, Tensleep and the sheriff "reached the road that tips up to the prairie, runnin' east and west." The lawman reins in and appears to think. "Our ways part here," he told me. "You are ridin' west. I think it best I forget you and that you forget me."

"Don't let 'em forget me entirely, will yuh, Sheriff?"

"You want me to keep alive any affection they might have for a renegade and a horse thief, Maxon?"

"Not at all," I tell him. "Just keep a kind of recollection of the sentimental fool who gits his pleasure hornin' into other folks' troubles."

"I'll do it," he says. "Then I'm ridin' west to whatever fate has in store for a hawss—er—trader. I'd gladly give my gunhand to enjoy for the rest of this cruel, rollickin' restless thing called life, a bit of peace."

THE THREE MESQUITEERS

What comes quickly to mind when you look at the above title? Most of us who grew up during the Thirties will never forget those so-called "Trigger Trios," who rode across the silver screen on those Saturday afternoons. The Range Busters, The Rough Riders, The Trail Blazers, and The Three Mesquiteers. What thrills they provided! Usually at the end the trio mounted their horses and went riding off down some main street or a lone trail leading toward the distant hills. Well, in the pulps it was quite often the same, as the reader will find out in due time. Here is the final part of a Three Mesquiteers epic, "Valley of the Scorpion," as featured in *Big-Book Western* magazine. The author was William Colt MacDonald: Muffled hoofbeats thudded across the sand, departing at a good lope. Silence fell over the group as they listened. No one spoke. Then Esteban touched Logan's arm. He pointed toward the north. There, sky-lighted on a rise of ground, the Three Mesquiteers had pulled their ponies to a halt and whirled for a last look at the group standing down in the hollow. Lullaby was on Tucson's right, Stony on the left. The three sat motionless for a moment, then as the final rays of the sun flung an aura of golden light over the trio, Tucson raised one arm, palm outward, in the Indian sign of peace. Crimson banners waved but a brief minute in the wstern sky, changed quickly to mauve, then gray, which in turn faded swiftly, along with the three figures, from view. A long drawn "ADIOS, AMIGOS-S-S—" floated clearly down the slope through the gathering purple twilight. Darkness dropped like a great soft blanket over the land. Then through the desert night came the steady drumming of horses' hoofs, the sound growing fainter and ever fainter, until the muted beats had blended imperceptibly into the gentle breeze that ruffled the sagebrush.

The West knew this trio by many names. Law officers termed them the best loved and at the same time the most feared trio in all the southwest. One old-timer said: "If they's any bounty ever put on Satan's pelt, Tucson Smith and his pards will shore collect it."

The trio was pictured thusly: The riders pulled their horses to a walk as they neared the center of town. To all appearances they were just a trio of drifting cowboys, loafing their way across country. They wore the identical garb, overall pants, vests over woolen shirts, bandannas knotted at their throats, high-heeled riding boots and rolled-brim Stetsons. Each carried two Colt .45's in the worn holsters that were attached to twin cartridge belts encircling their slim hips.

The three cowboy partners were usually described as follows: TUCSON SMITH had brick-red hair, a wide mouth, straight thin lips, a hooked nose and a square sinewy jaw in a sun-tanned bony face. Eyes, slate-gray "with humorous lights which could on occasion change swiftly to a hue of cold, blue steel." He was a rangy person, six feet tall and, like Brooke, carried beneath his shirt a brace of walnut-butted Colt .45's. Age, a trifle over 30. He usually sat astride a rangy sorrel gelding.

STONY BROOKE: Dark complected, snub-nosed, with innocent-looking blue eyes, a good–natured grin. He had wide shoulders and a barrel-like torso. He had a wide, mis-chievous-gargoyle grin. Age was 30 or thereabouts. Not quite as tall as the other two men. It was said, "He'd laugh at his own funeral." He showed no fear under fire.

LULLABY JOSLIN: About age 30, he stood not quite six feet tall, lanky, with bony-wristed long arms and light, drowsy hazel eyes. His leather-like features were long and "dourful looking, much like a scarecrow. He was sleepy-appearing and usually soft-spoken." He had straight black hair. His guns were swifter than greased lightning. He rode a black pony.

Here now are some scenes of the bullet trio in action: (1) Just inside the doorway stood Tucson Smith, Stony, and Lullaby, their thumbs hooked in cartridge belts, calmly surveying the gang. Then they leaped inside. Tucson's hands were spitting fire; Lullaby's hand belched a mushroom of flame and smoke.

(2) Then Tucson moved, an instant before the explosion came; catlike he threw his body to one side, rolled over and came up with one hand drawing his six-shooter. The gun roared once, twice, three times, the reports apparently blending into one continuous sound.

(3) Crack! A lead slug whistled viciously past Tucson's head. He uttered a sharp cry, flung his arms in the air, and slipped from the saddle. Stony and Lullaby swore violent oaths, unleased a flaming stream of lead at the ridge top. Tucson said quietly from his sprawled position on the hot sand, "He didn't hit me." A moment later Lullaby and Stony crouched at Tucson's side as though examining a wound. Lullaby went through the motions of tearing up a bandanna. Stony rose once, shook a clenched fist at the top of the ridge and again dropped at Tucson's side. The two turned him over. Tucson was talking all this time: "Now you two take your horses and mine. There's a slight roll of land a mile back. Go back past it as though you were headin' back to the nearest town for help."

"And leave you here?" Stony cut in.

"Listen, Stony, don't argue," Tucson pleaded from his face-down, motionless position on the earth. "We've got to trick that hombre some way."

"But suppose he shoots you when we leave?" asked Lullaby.

"I'll have to chance that. I don't think he will—"

Spat! A slug buried itself in the sand at Lullaby's side. Lullaby rose, shook his fist.

"You see," Tucson spoke earnestly, his face cradled on one arm, against the sand, "he'll keep on until he gets one of you. Go on now. Drift, pronto." He paused a moment. "Wait— you better pretend to examine me some more, so you can leave me in a position to watch the slope."

Then, reluctantly, Stony and Lullaby mounted.

Here is a sequence taken from "Winchester Welcome," March 1935 issue: Reaching to his right hip pocket, Glascow produced the handcuffs. Tucson took them with his left hand. Glascow's left hand reached to the other hip pocket, bringing into sight a bunch of heavy keys. Tucson was watching warily, left hand holding the handcuffs. "Here's the keys," Glascow muttered, backing away a pace. With his left hand he tossed them to Tucson, figuring to keep Tucson's right hand occupied. At the same instant Glascow's right hand darted for his holster. Deftly then, Tucson's right hand plucked the bunch of keys from the air. His left hand released hold of the handcuffs, stabbed toward his left holster before the cuffs had fallen to the earth. Even as the gun-muzzle cleared leather it commenced to belch smoke and white flame. Two slugs kicked up tiny clouds of dirt as Tucson's gun swept up to bear on Glascow's body. Glascow's six-shooter emitted one wild shot as he staggered back. His wide-spread legs were swept from under him as though by some huge invisible hand, and he went sprawling a half dozen paces away. Tucson backed two steps, holding his gun in readiness. Glascow went down, bracing himself on one hand, a look of hate drawing back his lips in a savage snarl. He raised his right hand, gripping the gun for a last attempt. Then came a burst of flame. Tucson swayed to one side, his own report blending with that of Glascow's. Glascow's body jerked. The gun fell from his weakening grasp. For a moment he braced himself on both hands, staring wildly at Tucson. Then his bulky form crumpled and he sank to the roadway.

Methodically, Tucson plugged out the empty shells in his gun cylinder, refilled the chambers with fresh loads. For an instance silence engulfed the long street. Tucson glanced across at the Red Bull Saloon. Chap Bell and another Box-8 puncher named Auringer stood on the porch. Both their hands were on gun-butts. Tucson eyed them steadily a momemt. "Want any of this?" he called across the street. Chap Bell didn't reply. Auringer shook his head. "It ain't any of our business," he replied. The two stepped quickly to the plank sidewalk and hurried away down the street.

ALAMO PAIGE

Exciting Western (A Thrilling Publication) featured a character, from the pen of author Reeve Walker, who went by the name of Alamo Paige. His first appearance was in the March 1941 issue. The story: "Paige of the Pony Express."

Like many of his counterparts who ended up working for Russell, Majors, and Waddell (including another pulp character named Freckles Malone), Alamo Paige was a pony express rider. He was one of those "rock-hard, small-built Texans," sometimes described in the stories as being wiry-built. He had ice-blue eyes, "his whip-muscled frame carrying around less than a hundred and twenty pounds." His muscle-corded back was hidden beneath his usual attire of smoky buckskins. He wore a Texas sombrero kept in place by a rawhide chin cord. A wide cowhide belt was

around his middle. It held a bowie knife and a single Colt .44 with a heavy walnut grip. As far as his age was concerned, he was described as "barely pass his majority."

He was another of those "Ace riders of the Pony Express" who kept company with the likes of one young hombre named Bill Cody, an express relief rider at the time. Cody was then only 14 years of age, and "his lean frame gave scant promise of the stature he was to attain later as Buffalo Bill."

The pony express station was located at the Bowie Joe Thornton Trading Post, a Wyoming outpost situated right at the mouth of the Hatcher River Canyon. Thornton, who served as stock tender, was a shaggy-maned giant of a man. He had a daughter, Texanna, who looked after the merchandise in the trading post most of the time. Texanna had hair that "resembled clusters of spun copper" and blue eyes. Alamo Paige once told her: "Yuh're might buena to me, Tex." Paige wished her father would take his daughter away before the Indians raided the place. For her part, each time Alamo leaped into the saddle for another mail run, Texanna "died a thousand deaths, wondering if he'd get through." She told him: "But I knew all along you would. You weren't born to lose your scalp to any Indian."

Here's a fact we were never aware of before that's worth passing along: a mail rider would often carry, as part of his equipment, a brass horn which hung from his neck. As the rider came within earshot of the relay station, he'd sound the horn. This would allow them to have another horse ready and waiting for the quick changeover. It was so written in Company regulations. Also, a rider did not carry a rifle. Everything was sacrificed in order to reduce the weight of both saddle and rider. The price charged for mail was five dollars an ounce.

Here is an incident from the first story: Canuck Bemont stepped into the room, highlights glittering on his cartridge belt and holstered Colts. Then his features drained of color as he recognized Alamo Paige standing there. Bemont's shaggy fists plummeted thighward and came up with six-guns that belched smoke and thundered into the log-walled room. Paige had anticipated that draw. But his first instinctive move was not to unholster his own .44. Instead, he lunged sideways in the split clock-tick of time that Bemont was snatching his Dragoon Colts from their holsters. His rush hurled him against Texanna Thornton, bearing the girl floorward as bullets screamed over the table top to flatten against the rock mantel of the fireplace. With Texanna safely below the line of fire, Paige kicked upward, his bootheel slamming against the underside of the table where he had been eating. Darkness plunged about the occupants of the trading past as the upsetting table knocked the lamp floorward with a tinkle of shattering glass. Scuttling lizardlike behind the paralyzed figures of Thornton and Captain Potter, Paige now got his own .44 from leather. But Bemont had already fled from the doorway, not daring to remain outlined against the starlit yard. Scrambling to his feet, Paige raced to the doorway. He was in time to see Bemont vault into the saddle of a horse, held for him by a whiskered companion. Then both outlaws rode away and headed off on the trail which zigzagged up Eagle Rock Mountain, south of the trading post.

From "Stage Line to Hell," October 1945, comes this bit of action: There was a burst of gunfire. Charging in, his Colt spitting flame alongside his horse's neck, Alamo felt the savage, primitive lust of battle. A bandit, kneeling in the road, was firing rapidly at him. Alama felt the kick of the gun in his hand, saw the bandit spin half around and sprawl in the dust. There was confusion in the road, with some of the outlaws standing to fight and others making a break for their horses. But the sheriff's men cut in and there was a surging struggle. Alamo swooped down on a tall bandit who had reached his horse and swung into the saddle. The outlaw whirled, gun in hand, and Alamo saw the features of Sylvan Brody beneath the slipped-down bandanna. Brody's gun flashed and the lead tugged sharply at the Express Rider's shirt. Alamo could have shot him pointblank then, but instead he drove his horse hard into the gambler's. The shock knocked Brody out of the saddle, as Alamo had intended, but the gambler did not lose his gun. Sprawling in the dusty roadway, he whipped around on one knee, brought up the gun to point directly in the face of the Express Rider looming over him. There was no choice. Alamo shot him, and saw his body flop back limply into the sand.

THE CIRCLE J PARDS

According to pulpologist Lester Belcher (who at this writing has almost a complete set of the above-named magazine), an individual named BILLY WEST was half owner of the Circle J Ranch. It was located in Twin Rivers, Montana. Billy's adopted sister, RUTH DAWE, was the other half.

Billy had some sidekicks on hand when the gunsmoke rolled. These were: JOE SCOTT, a redheaded hombre who rode a sorrel horse; BUCK "Squaredeal" FISTER, an old puncher with penetrating brown eyes and a walrus mustache; and a Chinese cook by the name of SING LO.

It seemed that Buck, Joe and Billy were called "The fightinest bunch in all of Montana." Billy usually rode astride a chestnut mare. As time went on, he was associated with the likes of Sonny Tabor, The Whistling Kid, Pete Rice, and Kid Wolf.

"There were," Belcher told me, and also wrote in the October 1983 issue of *Echoes Magazine,* "a total of 449 stories and 150 front covers of Billy West. Artist Robert G. Harris painted quite a number of those *Wild West* magazine covers."

The author of the stories was given as Cleve Endicott.

NAVAJO RAINE

Exciting Western had a series of stories written under the name of Jackson Cole. We know that to be a pseudonym, but have no clue as to the author's real name. He was a favorite of many readers.

Navajo Thomas Raine was often described as "a devil on horseback." Orphaned at age twelve during the Tonto Basin War, he was forced to flee into the mountains after his father, Marshal Powder Raine, was killed in a gun trap. The boy was subsequently found by the Navajoes, almost dead from exposure. They nursed him back to health. He grew to manhood under Indian tutelage, and eventually was asked by Captain Burt Mossman to join the Arizona Territorial Rangers. In one of the stories Navajo explained the incident involving his father: "During the Tonto Basin War my father, Marshal Raine, was killed by bushwhackers. The men who murdered him thought he told me their

names, since he made it home before he died. The killers tried to nab me, but I skinned out for the mountains. I was just a button, and would have died of the cold and hunger if the Navajoes hadn't found me and taken me in."

He was usually seen as tall, lean, sinewy, with dark skin burned by desert winds and sun, and queer greenish eyes. Those eyes were often like polished jade, bright, hard, cold. He had a flat stomach, deep chest, shoulders broad and square. He wore his dark hair long enough that it curled against his shoulders. So, with his rather hawkish dark features and heavy black hair, he was often mistaken for an Indian, something he did not resent. His attire was partly cowboy, partly Indian scout. He wore a flat-crowned hat, a black Stetson with a string of turquoise and silver ornaments around the crown. At his belt swung a pair of tied-down holsters that held two long-barreled, well balanced six-shooters with turquoise-silver butts. These were a gift from his Indian blood brothers. Rangers usually worked in pairs, but not Raine. He never called for aid except that offered by his own guns. His spurs were also turquoise-studded silver. His high-heeled boots were black. Raine was a crack shot with either .45's or long guns, an expert with a knife or his fists. He could "talk like an Indian, reason like a lawyer, deal out justice like a judge, and had a mountain lion's courage."

He also had a keen mind and flawless character sense. This quick ability to judge both Indians and whites had stood him in good stead more than once in the difficult job of bringing law to this wild and savage frontier. As a result he was hated and feared by renegades throughout the mountain country. As time went on, he became more deadly than his renowned father, the Marshal, had been. He rode a magnificent blue roan gelding called Wampum. The horse for once seemed rather ordinary and not in the same class with Saber of the Rio Kid or Goldy belonging to Ranger Jim Hatfield, or Shadow, the property of Walt Slade. Raine would also talk to Wampum, but not as much as some other riders we've run across.

Here now are some views of Raine's ability with guns: Raine's big shoulders swayed, his lean hands whipping down in a motion that ended with the bellowing roar of a .45 Colt. Al Stewart fell backwards, an eerie wail running from his sagging mouth, blood springing from a bullet hole squarely between his yellow eyes. The six-shooter spun out of his dying hand, still uncocked. Raine swung his gun fast, for Tuck Stewart was buying chips in the deadly game. The ranger staggered when smoking lead ripped across his side, missing clean with a slug from each of his turquoise-butted guns. Before he could get his balance and fire again, Tuck Stewart's second shot ripped his right temple, knocking him off his feet. "Take it, yuh green-eyed son!" Tuck Stewart bawled, and bounced in close, smoking gun slanting down for the kill. Raine wasted no time in attempting to get on his feet. He slanted his guns up from the floor, smoke and flame and ear-jarring thunder running steadily from their muzzles. Tuck Stewart thumbed both guns, but the slugs they threw passed a foot too high above Raine's blood-drenched face to be dangerous. Stewart was bending backwards in a series of short, jerky motions, each spasmodic twitch telling of a bullet smashing through his big body. Raine quit firing when Tuck Stewart's bullet-torn, bloody hulk slammed to the floor. "Jumpin' Jehoshaphat!" Sheriff Buck Glover's voice was a croaking whisper. "I reckon that ends the trouble here in Three Sleep Basin." He watched as Raine went limping out the door. The sheriff, Raine decided, could sweep out his own office—dead thieves, dust and all!

Here is another sequence: His slim thumbs snapped out of the shell belts, and his hands were blurred shadows that smothered the bright gleam of silver and turquoise gun grips. Twin jets of flame-tipped smoke spread out from his thighs, and Tex Sharbin died even as he drew his guns.

Raine was one of those roll-your-own smokers. He would often carry a piece of wire in one buckskin pocket and use it now and then to pick a few locks. (One example can be found in "Navajo Reads Signs," February 1946 issue.) Sometimes before he bedded down for the night in a cabin, Raine crumpled up sheets of paper and scattered them about his bunk, so that their rattle might betray any intruder who came in the dark. His Indian upbringing and tutelage had enabled him to read signs as well as any redman.

Incidentally, the story titles were interesting and different. There was, for instance: "Have A Harp"; "Put the Lid On, Ranger"; "Ranger's Ride With Death." There is one story that has eluded us, titled "Rawhide Ranger," in which Navajo teams up with none other than Steve Reese of the Range Riders. The date was February 1944. One ardent Raine follower wrote, saying that "I gotta have it. Gotta have it." In the story the two forces combine to clean up a renegade crew of high-grading outlaws. Perhaps we'll find it one day soon and can tell readers about it!

One of the most famous heroes of all time to be featured in the pulps was probably the one who gave his name to *The Lone Ranger* magazine. Unfortunately there were only eight issues. They are as follows: "The Phantom Rider," April 1937; "The Masked Rider's Justice," May 1937; "Killer Roundup," June 1937; "Valley of the Shadows," July 1937; "The Cave of Terror," August 1937; "Heritage of the Plains," September 1937; "Lone Star Renegade," October 1937; "Death's Head Vengeance," November 1937.

The magazine was published by Trojan Publishing Company, Chicago. Cost was ten cents. The author of the stories was never listed, but most believe it was Fran Striker. In his excellent book, "His Typewriter Wore Spurs," authored by Fran Striker, Jr., there is (on page 136) a picture of the first pulp issue. Also (on page 137) is the comment—"LR "Dime" pulp novels started." On the book's flyleaf, the son wrote these words to me: "Thanks for your interesting letter and the interest in my dad's work and life."

The covers of all issues we saw were extremely well done. Excellent interior sketches were used abundantly in each story. An artist identified as Kidd did the first cover, while H.J. Ward was identified with the others we previewed.

The Lone Ranger is described as follows: He was tall, about six feet two, lean and sinewy with broad shoulders, a firm, tanned chin and well-formed mouth. He possessed a soft, deep, resonant voice, usually speaking in a clipped, precise manner, quite different from the usual drawling style of the country. He gave one the impression of calm deliberation. His grim, strong personality was much in evidence.

This was that mysterious individual whose face had, with one exception, been seen by only one living man. That exception was Tonto, his faithful Indian companion. Together with Silver, the beautiful silver-white stallion ridden by the Lone Ranger, they had acquired fame that was legendary throughout the length and breadth of the West. All three, two men and a horse, acted together with a smooth precision that came only from long association and deep mutual understanding. True, there were times when that mask had to be removed, but in such cases stains made from berries, roots and herbs were used to change his face.

In "The Phantom Rider" we are given this view: With a wide sombrero pulled low over the mask on this face, a man rode through the night. His slender figure of whipcord strength forked the silver-white stallion beneath him with the easy grace of a panther, and panther-like, through the slits of his mask, his steel-gray eyes studied the ground ahead when scudding clouds uucovered the face of the moon.

TONTO had been a companion of the white man for many years, and had faced all manner of danger in helping the Masked Rider mete out justice in the early West. Few men had a better grasp of the habits of nature and its creatures. In combat, the Indian was a tower of strength. He could throw a knife with a speed that almost equaled the Lone Ranger's gunplay. His white stallion, White Feller, along with Silver had been trained to react to certain voice commands from the Masked Man: "Play dead!" the Lone Ranger shouted. Both stallions flopped prone on the ground and remained motionless.

Tonto, who often wore a buckskin shirt and fringed trousers, was described thusly: He was bronzed, with a high-cheekboned face, hair straight and long, which fell beneath a bit of red cloth drawn tight around his forehead. He was a Pottowatomie Indian. In every way he was like his Indian brothers except in the expression of his face. It was a more intelligent face, a rare tolerant expression that other red men did not possess. His long association with the Lone Ranger had given him a character that combined the best features of both red men and white.

Here is a scene from the first story: With a shout Tonto dropped from the tree, landing squarely on the back of one of the outlaws. His fist swung hard to meet a bristling jaw. Shouts of rage came from the throats of the surprised men. The Lone Ranger, quick to see the situation, thundered, "Come on, Silver!" and the great horse charged. Scar swung his gun and squeezed the trigger point blank at Tonto, who was locked in the arms of two men. At the moment the gun exploded, the flying hoofs of Silver struck at the outlaw. His shot went wild, and his gun went flying. "At them, Silver, old boy!' shouted the Masked Rider to the stallion. A gun clutched in his hand served as a club to crack down on the cursing outlaws. Hands tugged at the Lone Ranger, pulling him from his horse. Desperately he struck at the unknown attacker, missed, then saw a gleaming knife, the same that had struck Old Joe, being brought into play. A cruel face leered close, as the arms of the Lone Ranger were pinned by the man behind him. Once again Silver reared, and with a fury like that of a wild horse that never knew taming, his forelegs rose and fell, and hard hoofs lashed the knife wielder to the ground. Tonto broke free, and another blow from his hard-thrown fist landed flush on the jaw of the one who held the masked man's arms. "Break clear," shouted the Lone Ranger to Tonto. "Silver," he shouted to his horse. For a split second all three were free of the clutches of the outlaws, who were gathering themselves for a rush that would have ended the desperate fight. The Lone Ranger leaped to the back of Silver, shouted a warning to the understanding Tonto. Then came that cry that sent the silver stallion away at lightning pace, the cry that rang throughout the West: "Heigh Yo, Silver!"

A flash, a thunder of hoofs in fast tattoo and the Lone Ranger and Tonto, both riding on Silver, disappeared into the darkness.

Here is a sequence called to my attention by pulpologist Dick Myers. It is from the novel "Killer Roundup": The noon sun of the San Juan Mountains was blistering hot in a copper sky. In the lead was a rider with a bronzed face, dark eyes and high cheekbones. It was Tonto, friend and companion of the Lone Ranger. Behind him on another stallion, larger and more powerful, rode a tall, slender man, whose face was concealed by a mask. The steel-gray eyes peering easily through the slits of the mask watched the trail ahead. He sat on his horse easily, his body moving with the grace of a leopard or panther with each movement of the powerful white stallion.

From that same story, another vivid passage: "Stand away from the girl!" It was a crisp, commanding voice, each word clipped short. Harve dropped his arms, and his right hand flashed toward his gun. "If you think you can beat me to the draw," the Lone Ranger said, "you're welcome to try." Harve cursed, and his gun flashed up. Two guns roared together, orange flame lashing out. Harve Morgan's gun jumped with the smash of the Lone Ranger's bullet. It spun through the air to land fully ten feet distant.

Author Fran Striker had a way with words when it came to description.

Take this example: She was trim of figure, small, blond. . ."Her arms were bare to the elbows, and a soft white shirt was open at the throat. Her pert little nose was shiny and her hair a tousled unruly mass of curls. It was not until she spoke that she was noticed. A single word, accompanied by the stamp of a small foot, brought four pairs of eyes focused on her. "Well?" said Sally Whitcomb. The effect was instant. Walrus was the first to recover, partly because he was the oldest and therefore the most nearly immune to female charms. "My Gawd, she's got men's pants on!" he gasped.

In the final analysis most readers probably remember reading the following more than any other scene. It just has a way of forming a wonderful picture in one's mind: Then the tall masked man's foot hit the stirrup, the white stallion leaped into action. A ringing cry accompanied those pounding hoofs as the Lone Ranger settled in the saddle: HEIGH YO, SILVER!

A Thrilling Publication, issued every other month by Better Publications, Inc., cost: fifteen cents. Earlier issues were published by Ranger Publications, Inc. Many different authors wrote the stories, including Walker A. Tompkins, Gunnison Steele, Hascal Giles, Johnston McCulley—to list just a few.

The Ranger Riders were "range detectives" by profession, a triumvirate of hard-riding, fast-shooting lawmen, known from Canada to Mexico. The three men were under the direct command of Colonel George Beauvine, head of the Cattleman's Protective Association, with headquarters in Austin, Texas. He had a comfortable office with a view of the city from one of the windows. When seated at his desk he could press a button beneath the ledge to summon his secretary, a lean and wiry little man.

STEVE REESE was field chief of the CPA and leader of the Range Riders. He was a former St. Louis police lieutenant, a college graduate, who gave up city life for a career on the frontier. In his 30s, he had black hair just beginning to gray at the temples. This served to give him a distinguished appearance which few men of his age acquired. His eyes, black, penetrating, dark, were like furbished gunmetal. They often held a twinkle of amusement. A rather tall, broad-shouldered man, lean, with a muscular build, Reese was a formidable fighter with his fists as well as his guns. Twin .38's swung against his hips in holsters limbered and black with use. In the guise of an ordinary cowpoke he would use the vernacular when speaking.

The second member of the trio, JOSHUA JEREMIAH "DUSTY" TRAIL, a hombre who had a great desire and fondness for five-cent cigars, managed to carry a good supply no matter where he went on assignment. He was short, rotund, and his eyes "beneath their drooping-lids gaze did seem to give him a sleepy-lazy appearance." His eyes were blue. But his "fat" was all muscle, and he was unbelievably fast with a six-gun.

The third Range Rider, HENRY "HANK" BASCOM BALL was a fiery redhead, his face garnished with rust-red freckles. He was a favorite with the ladies. He was lean and lanky, a superb fighting machine, wild, reckless, loyal. He wore his guns low, as did Dusty Trail, and he pulled them fast. (Both men called Reese "Doc," a name they bestowed on him because of his methodical way of attacking the scourge of lawlessness. Usually idle banter would pass between Ball and Trail. It was a sort of hobby between them. Even if one had displayed anger now and then, it would have been dangerous to choose sides. They were bosom friends, one of whom would fight for the other at the drop of a hat.

Here is a sequence taken from "Feast of Flaming Guns," December 1945, by Johnston McCulley: Reese had drawn his feet back as he spoke. And now he came to them as if shot up by a steel spring. With lightning speed, he clawed his guns from their holsters, and before the man in front of the table could draw a breath he found himself looking at twin muzzles which seemed at that moment to be as large as the mouths of cannon. Dusty had braced hmself the moment he had seen Reese's sudden move, and his hand had dropped to his holster. But Doc Reese did not need any help to handle this hombre.

We have this bit from "Ghost Killers of Skull River," February 1946, by Gunnison Steele: The breath went out of Ivor. He stumbled backwards, and Reese hit him twice more in the face, two hard, chopping blows, and watched him fall to the ground. Reese stepped back, a warning of danger like a bell ringing in his brain, His eyes lifted to Ivor's riders, his own hands hovering over the twin .38s. Amazement was on their hard faces. They sat silently, their own hands near their guns, staring at Reese. Ivor was sitting up. Dusty Trail's cigar was clenched hard between his teeth. He was watching Steve Reese. His pudgy hands rested steadily on the butt of his gun. Steve Reese knew the peril of his position. He could beat any of those he faced to the draw—might even kill half of them before they killed him. But a gunfight against such odds could have but one possible ending. "I'll kill yuh for that, Reese!" Ivor said thickly.

"There's yore gun, boss, over there on the ground," a rider growled.

"Let the gun alone, Ivor," Reese said coldly. "Touch it and I'll kill yuh!"

"Go to it, boss!" the rider urged. "We'll cut him down if he touches a gun!"

Dusty Trail braced himself in the saddle and his finger curled about the trigger of his gun. He knew that, in order to save his chief, he couldn't wait a second longer to show his hand. Dusty had already started his draw when his blue eyes widened and became riveted on a spot directly behind Ivor and his hard case riders. His sigh of relief was almost a groan.

"Freeze, yuh polecats! If yuh don't, I'll spoil this whole valley with yore smell!" a voice said flatly. Ivor's men, reading stark menace in that cold voice, "froze."

Hank Ball spurred from the dense timber behind the riders, a long-barreled gun in each hand. Steve Reese snatched out his own guns, while Dusty Trail, almost unable to suppress a wide grin, sat back in the saddle and eased his hand away from his weapon. Reese had been aware of the red-haired Hank Ball's presence, even before Dusty was. Then Reese spoke to the sullen riders: "Unbuckle yore gunbelts and drop 'em to the ground, slow and careful."

The reader will recall we mentioned author Hascal Giles earlier. Here are a few of the other pulp magazines to feature his by-line: *Ace High, Action Stories, Big Book Western, Best Western, Blue Book, Complete Western Book, Exciting Western, Fifteen Western Tales, Five Western Novels, Giant Western, Lariat Story Magazine, Popular Western, Rangeland Romances, Story Annual, New Western, Western Rangers,* and *Western Short Stories.* Giles sold his first western story when he was a high school senior and "kept at it, off and on, until the pulps began to fade away in the late Fifties."

Incidentally, Giles expresses a definite fascination for an area known as Monument Valley.

Here are some scenes from his Range Riders story "Sign of the Straddle Bug," May 1948: The towering hooded spokesman dropped his hand in a blur of speed, dragging free his holstered gun. It was a lightning-fast move, but Reese's keen eyes had seen the draw born in the tightening of the man's wrist muscles. Reese's right-hand Colt barked harshly, and the man's gun spun away with the explosion. The leader yelped in pain, ramming his stinging fingers under his armpit for comfort. The others threw their weapons down in despair, raising their hands in surrender as Reese gestured with his Colt. "That could have been closer, mister," Reese said angrily. "Now cut the man down like I said. The rest of you stand hitched. Don't get any ideas, because you can't even guess how many men I've got in the brush around you."

(2) Charlie Claw grunted in surprise, swung a smashing fist at the point of Reese's square chin. But the chin was not there when the blow swished past. Reese ducked like a bobbing swallow, his head coming up under Claw's guarding left. He rammed his right fist savagely into Charlie Claw's middle, bending the man over and driving him back with the wind swooshing out of his lungs.

The savage speed of Reese's attack made it a brief fight. Before Claw could recover his wind, the field chief bent swiftly and scooped up the fallen gun. Claw straightened and started forward, drawing up short when he saw the bore of his own Colt staring him in the face. "Well, I'll be a—"

"You'll be a dead duck if yuh move!" Reese told him.

(3) While the horse drank from the brackish pond, Reese took time to check the loads in the twin .38 Colts that rode low on his thighs. He loosened the guns in their casings, twirled the cylinder of each to dislodge any dust in the mechanism, and then dropped them lightly back into place. There was nothing around him but a heat-buzzing silence; still the stifling air seemed charged with an electric tenseness. Somewhere ahead of Reese lurked danger and mystery—men who hid their faces in shielding hoods and left a straddle bug mark where their victiims died. Foreboding rode the saddle with the dark-haired field chief as he pulled away from the water hole and plunged into the rocks. Had Reese known what awaited him there, he would never have replaced his guns. For he rounded a jagged granite heap a moment later and rode straight into the face of grinning death.

Steve Reese

Hank Ball

Dusty Trail

A Popular Publication, issued bi-monthly; cost: fifteen cents. Covers and interior illustrations among the best. The author: Stone Cody.

El Halcon de la Sierra! The Great Hawk of the Sierras! One with the power and mind far beyond other men. But at the same time there was a clean decency, a warmth, some intangible, magnetic thing which changed the careless glance into something close to adoration. He also possessed a super-normal sensitiveness and acute night vision few other men had. He could easily see objects in the darkness. But the clarity of his own night vision was in some way a disadvantage, for he could never quite believe that a shadow could conceal him from other men's eyes. To him the night was not black but gray. There were even colors in it— deep blues and silver and black and purples and faint lavenders, and all the shades between, and the yellow glint of starlight like a luminescence in the air. He was amazed.

Silver Trent was a man perfectly proportioned; he did not look his size. Power vibrated from the easy, great-muscle stance of his body and the lean, glowing lines of his face, as he laughed out of the depths of his gray-blue eyes. These were warm and luminous, and they sparkled above a predatory beak of a nose. He had a wide, sloping shoulder, panther-like, powerful and strong. Feral white teeth showed in a grin that stretched the mobile, chiseled lips of a generous mouth.

Silver Trent's girl was a slender, dark haired, blue-eyed lass named Gracia. She was always getting into some kind of tdrouble. Once she was kidnapped by El Diablo and spirited away to a wasteland stronghold. Trent had quite a time of it going to her rescue.

Trent was given assistance by a group of men known as the Hawks. Their battle cry: "A nos ostros Los Halcones!" (Hell Hawks for Trent!) Among the members were:

Ricardo, of the swagger and the lean, sunlit face.

Doc Brimstone, the medico-Americano, with his hearty belly and great empurpled beak of a nose.

Bignose Beaujolais, the hombre with a wooden leg and a proboscis that outrivaled the doctor's.

Pablo the Pious, whose only drunkeness was war. In battle he became a cursing madman whose inspired and gargantuan blasphemies had become a legend in the land.

Lars Johanssen, a huge blond man with shoulders like that of a bull. He was even bigger than Silver Trent.

Magpie Myers, with a yellow-stained mustache that was really white, an ageless wrinkled-leather face. He was Apache-trained and could move "like a ghost."

<u>Jim Clane</u> and <u>Beau Buchanan</u>, both very fast on the draw. Beau was a poker-faced gambler and one who could read trail signs. But probably Clane had the edge with a gun, for his appreciation of a six-gun was like a man's cognition of the inner secrets of his own heart. Also in the group were <u>Leon Costillo</u>, <u>Basilip</u>, the hunchback, and <u>Gomez</u>, the man with a scarred face. One individual, <u>Juan Beixos</u>, was killed during a gun battle. The last person to aid Trent was known as <u>Padre Pete</u>.

Here is an example of the draw made by Jim Clane: His right hand blurred to his thigh, whipped up, iron-freighted. His movement was so fast that the eye could not follow it—until the eased-back hammer of the weapon slapped downward and the gun spat flame, roaring.

Compare that to the draw of Silver Trent: With a curious regret he knew he must kill this man. His right hand flicked like a lizard's tongue licking a fly, and blasted flame and thunder.

From the novel "Gun-Carr for the Lost Legion" comes this: "Power showed in him—vibrated from the easy, great-muscled stance of his body, lay easily, almost lazily, along the lean, glowing lines of his face, laughed out of the depths of his eyes. Power of mind and body beyond other men."

Once someone asked: "Do you mean you are of the Hawks?"

"I am what I am," Silver replied.

When it came to disguising himself, Trent did a fairly good job, as we see in this segment: He was a big man—too big, almost, for a Mexican. He was dressed in a pair of ragged cotton pants, a shirt which had seen better days, and a tall straw sombrero. His skin, face, hands and feet, which were bare, were Indian-brown. He drove a burro before him and carried a guitar on his back.

"Dios!" the innkeeper muttered to himself. "A minstrel, and in this country! Truly, these days bring me strange sights."

"What did you say?" Eyes, gray-black, held him steadily.

"I say you are welcome, hombre."

Silver followed him. This disguise of his, he saw, did poorly even in this light of sunset. Yet it was the best he had been able to improvise at the hut of the goatherd he had found at the edge of the hills that surrounded the valley.

When the magazine reached trail's end, Silver Trent and his band found a new home in *Star Western Magazine*. All of this was fully explained in the August 1937 issue, in a segment titled "Up the Trail," found on page 139. We also ran down the February 1941 issue of *Star Western* and a story called "One Last Raid for Trent's Hell Hawks." In this epic it seemed Magpie (really Ben Myers—sometimes spelled Meyers) had run into a heap of trouble down Tucson way, got himself shot and ended up in jail. There was also a stage holdup, with Trent's bunch accused. Magpie through an old friend named Dave was able to get word to Trent. As you might expect, Trent and his bunch showed up in the hills just northwest of Tucson. Here is how Trent was pictured: "A man stood there with a gun in his hand. He was big, with wide, powerful shoulders which shaped down to make almost a V at his waist. His square-cut weathered features were set hard just now, and his eyes, dark gray in the lamplight, looked like glacier ice at the close of a wintry day."

Incidentally, Trent was sometimes knows as the Rio Robin Hood.

SILVER TRENT

PADRE PETE

GRACIA

Hicks

Butler

PETE RICE

This was another Street & Smith magazine. The author was listed as Austin Gridley, a house-name of course. His real name was Ben Conlon. According to John Dinan, Rice "was more of a modern detective than a rootin'-tootin' pulp cowboy, as crimes and circumstances surrounding them were modern and not particularly western."

Pulpologist Link Huller said that "Rice was not a typical western lawman. Nor were his adventures typical of those found in western pulp magazines. There was a strong emphasis on mystery, with Rice serving as a very capable detective." Huller backs up Dinan's statement by adding "The stories took place in the modern west, with the reader encountering airplanes, automobiles, telephones, and other examples of the Twentieth Century."

At first it was titled *Pete Rice Magazine,* then in time changed to *Pete Rice Western Adventures.* He also appeared in *Wild West Weekly,* in what was known as the "cross-over." Pete's adventures were chronicled in the pulps from 1933 to 1939.

Author Ron Goulart, writing in his book *Cheap Thrills,* stated that "the *Pete Rice Magazine* was built around a cowboy with a coterie of distinctive sidekicks. Street & Smith hoped he'd do as well as Doc Savage and his distinctive sidekicks, but he didn't."

PETE RICE was Sheriff of Buzzard Gap, Arizona, and the law in Trinchers County, and was known throughout the Southwest as a famous peace officer. He carried the nickname of "Pistol Pete." He lived with his mother (the only person he loved more than the law itself) in a flower-covered cottage out on the edge of town. She had silver hair and gray eyes, and kept his pearl-handled guns cleaned and well oiled. As pulpologist Robert Sampson put it, "Pete Rice was a gum-chewing sheriff who lived in a sugar-coated little house decorated with cupids."

Another member of the team was Vulcan, an English Mastiff. Rice rode a sorrel named Sonny, and called the horse his "four-legged deputy." In his article, "The Law in Trinchers County," Huller states that "the powerful, magnificent sorrel had a star-shaped blotch of white in the center of his forehead—his badge of office."

Rice had his office in the back of a Buzzard Gap barber shop. He was sided by two part-time deputies, LAWRENCE MICHAEL "Misery" HICKS, and WILLIAM ALAMO "Teeny" BUTLER.

Hicks, a homely, wrinkled-faced man with blue eyes, was afraid of absolutely nothing that walked. He had a scrawny, undersized body and weighed only one hundred and twenty pounds. He spoke with a slightly nasal twang. He ran the barber shop where Rice kept his office. On the side, Misery sold bottles of his home-made remedy-medicine for coughs, croups, chills, and the like. He also did his own brand of doctoring on the side. He rode a strawberry roan. His favorite weapons were his <u>bolas</u>, the gift of a roving Argentine cowpoke. (These were three rawhide thongs weighted with metal balls.) He was also pretty good with a gun.

Butler, on the other hand, was a Texan and just about the biggest man in the entire county. At six feet four, he even towered over Rice. He weighed three hundred pounds, but had little fat on his frame. He was an expert with a bull whip and rode a big bay horse.

Now Pete Rice was considered to be "an easy-going hombre—until the law was broken." Misery Hicks often left a customer sitting in his barber chair unshaven when Rice issued the call to come running. Teeny Butler was very slow to become angry, but once aroused, you'd best stand aside and look out. Often when Rice and Butler were pinned down by gunfire, they would "do their talking in sign language."

Here is a short paragraph from one of the stories: There were two sharp rifle reports. Two streaks of red flame knifed out from the moundlike swell of rocks. Slugs whined over the lawmen's heads. They dropped to the ground, and their hands clawed for their .45's. Another streak of rifle flame tongued out from the mound. The lawmen were prepared for a stiff battle—against just what odds, they could not know.

(On another page you will find reproductions of covers from the artist hands of Walter M. Baumhofer and Robert G. Harris. We hope you enjoy them.)

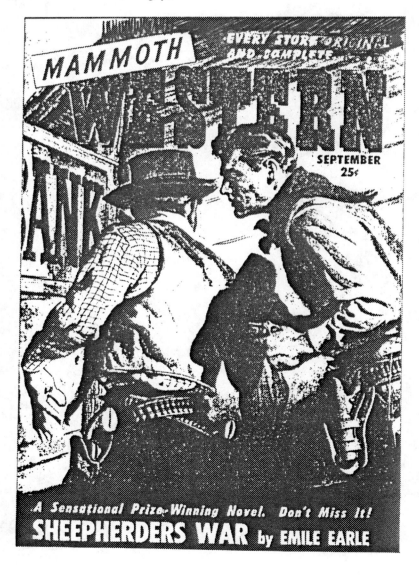

77

(The above cover, signed by Walter M. Baumhofer, hangs in the study of the author's Arizona hacienda. It was picked for us by artist Franklyn Hamilton from among a few proofs that Baumhofer had given to Frank.)

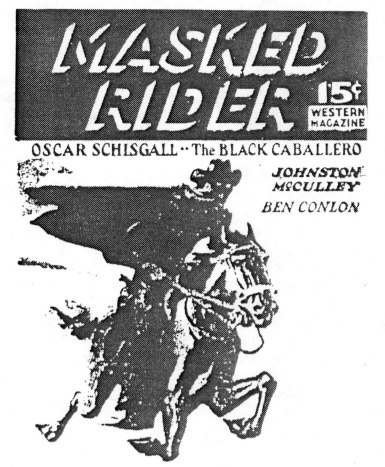

We have pictured above a very rare pulp, the first issue of *The Masked Rider Western,* April of 1934. It was published by Ranger Publications, Inc. On the contents page is written: He knew what it was to ride the lonely trail of the condemned, the cruel, imperilled existence of an outaw—the hunted mortal whose horse must ride with the wind, and whose life is no longer than his trigger finger. They called him the Robin Hood of the West. In some parts of Texas he was regarded as a myth rather than a reality. Here now is just a part of one scene: "In the deepest shadows of a few cottonwoods he stopped his horse. His eyes, flaming through twin slits in a black cloth, fixed their gaze on the isolated building. His clothing presented a perfect symphony in black. From sombrero to boots, including his mask, his apparel was absolutely uncompromising in its blackness. He wore a long cloak which flowered over him in voluminous black folds. When he rode fast it billowed out behind him like the wings of a bat."

The stallion itself shared the color—a mount as glossy black as a Nedja colt. Here is a part of the novel "Outlaws of Black Gold Butte" (June of 1937), as written by Ray Palmer Tracy: The figure was tall, with lean, hard lines that a voluminous black cape failed to conceal. A big black hat with soft, expensive curves shaded a hard face already concealed by a black hood. He stood quietly, seeming to be a statue carved from opaque hues of the night itself. The stars spangling the black sky, at that high altitude, seemed larger and more brilliant than at lower levels. They seemed to gleam with a bluer, colder flame. The hard keeness of them was reflected through slits in the black mask of the Rider as he studied the scene below him. With the slightest of rustles, the Rider turned up the slope. Over the ridge he stopped and gave a low whistle. There was movement within a small cluster of shivering quakies. Out stepped a black stallion. On feet light and sure as a cat's he trotted to his master. A swing of a lean, hard leg and the Rider was in the saddle. The holsters of a pair of black-handled guns gave his thighs a leathery slap. He gathered reins in black-gloved hands and the great horse moved up the

Uplift with a movement as flowing as the breeze.

As time went on some changes took place: "He drew forth a black sombrero, then shook out a somber black cloak and fastened it around his shoulders. A black domino mask completed the attire."

The Masked Rider was in reality cowpoke WAYNE MORGAN, who wandered from place to place. He was tall, wide-shouldered, firm of face, narrow-eyed, dark-haired. He had a fine, deep-chested physique. He weighed around one hundred and seventy pounds. He was a roll-your-own cigarette smoker. As Morgan he often looked like this: Dark-colored levis were thrust into the tops of worn cowboy boots. His blue shirt was like that worn by any other ranny, as was the bright neckerchief that he knotted loosely around his strong throat. The two heavy Colt .45's in their holsters were tied low on his hips.

Here is another view: "In spite of the throngs he had no difficulty, for people unconsciously stepped out of the way of this tall and broad-shouldered man. There was a certain air about him. He wore a pair of black-butted six-shooters in well-oiled holsters, but he wore them without ostentation. They seemed a part of the man."

Wayne Morgan's constant companion was BLUE HAWK, a Mexican-Yaqui Indian, lithe, erect, middle-aged, with raven black hair, face of copper-hue tint. He spoke with an accent common below the Mexican border. He had at one time attended a Mission School and had taken their teachings seriously. In his heart was a deep hatred for evil and injustice, accompanied by a fierce determination to fight for the honest and down-trodden. He was an expert with the rifle and the long-bladed knife. Blue Hawk had the keen perception of his people, along with trail instincts no white man could hope to develop in a whole lifetime.

Wayne Morgan had this philosophy: "I like to see justice done, even if my way o' gettin' it ain't always the way of the law."

One woman asked the Masked Rider: "Who are you anyway?"

"Just think of me as the Masked Rider, ma'am. The rest don't matter to nobody in this world—exceptin' myself."

Later on the magazine was published by Pines Publications, Limited (a Thrilling Publication). Throughout the series, different authors contributed. Author John Dinan, in *The Pulp Western*, wrote that "The later Masked Rider stories played down the eerie effects that Schisgall achieved in the earlier stories."

In his "A Time of Lively Fiction," author Robert Sampson wrote: "Subsequent characters drew liberally from The Lone Ranger image first appearing on 1933 radio and they lasted much longer. The most blatant swipe was THE MASKED RIDER—named Wayne Morgan, a good fellow, unjustly outlawed, who wore a mask, rode a horse named Midnight, and palled around with Blue Hawk, a Yaqui Indian."

Perhaps the reader might be interested in a typical story ending. Here is one from "The Range Wreckers," by Gunnison Steele, October 1946: Blue Hawk had been standing silently near the doorway, and now the Yaqui turned and slipped out into the night. The masked man followed him to the door, turned and lifted his hand. In his deep tones, he said: "Adios, friends!" then his black-clad figure also vanished silently into the shadows. A moment later the listeners inside the cabin heard the receding hoofbeats of two horses. Prosperous days were ahead for Sapphire Valley. But on other ranges crime and death were in the saddle. Troubled men were calling, raising their voices against injustice and intolerance. The tall, dark-clad rider mounted on the great black stallion and his faithful Yaqui trail-mate, Blue Hawk, rode through the night, ready as always to answer that call.

In our western collection is "Land of Big Timber," December 1947, written by none other than Hascal Giles. Here is a brief look at one particular incident: Riding at breakneck speed, the famed Robin Hood outlaw raced madly down the dangerous trail, his black sombrero pulled back by the breeze as the stallion Midnight galloped down the rocky hillside. As he rode, the masked man kept his eyes on the dangling figure of the grizzled driver who slipped closer to death at each turn of the wheels. At the same time, he guided the glistening black stallion closer to the rocking vehicle, striving to reach the horses before they came to the hairpin curve at the bottom of Wildcat Pass.

Midnight closed the gap like a racer, carrying his famed master alongside the driver's box. In one great leap, the masked man left the saddle and landed on the seat of the stage. He tottered fearfully a moment, the black cape whipping around his lithe frame. Then he fell forward on his hands and knees, caught his balance, and dragged the wounded driver back to safety.

15¢ STREET & SMITH'S

AUG. 5. 1933

Western Story

Magazine   EVERY WEEK

COMPLETE
BOOK-LENGTH
NOVEL
BY
MAX
BRAND

SILVERTIP

"I never seen Silvertip no more'n I ever seen wire gold. But I've heard gents talk about him here and there. He gets his name from a couple of streaks of gray hair over his temples, but he ain't old. He ain't thirty. He's ripped the top ground off a fortune twenty times, but he never stops long enough to dig out the pay dirt, because he's always in a hurry. Trouble is what he hunts for breakfast and kills for lunch, and eats for supper."

His real name was Jim Silver, and he was a man who traveled with just a blanket, slicker, rifle, salt and matches, in addition to what he wore on his back. "When I move, I generally have to move fast—and sometimes far," he said. Some thought a man like him could never find happiness in any one spot, there-fore he roved endlessly. Silver was one of those who fight their battles only once and for-get the past before their guns were cold. His philosophy was: "Wherever you go, no matter on what desert, there's always life of some sort. There aren't many desert jack rabbits, but there are some. You'll find game if you hunt carefully for it. And if you miss food for a couple of days, it makes it taste all the better when you make a kill."

As time went on people began to know his face. His picture had gotten into the newspa-per and magazines. Some fool had written about him, but told it all wrong and gilded him brighter than gold. He had managed to wade far enough into the reading of the book to be bogged down with the lies that were told. He knew he had become, in spite of himself, a public figure. His reputation had ridden further than Jim Silver had ever gone. Silver was a man who could pick up a two-hundred pound sack of potatoes with relative ease. "He'd go into the dark of a hole in the ground," one man said, "and rip the heart out of a mountain lion with his bare hands. I've seen quarters thrown up in the air, spinning, and I've seen him shoot 'em with never a miss." He was good with his left hand as well as his right. He had a habit of carrying some strong twine in his pocket. He was a smoker, as we learn in this sequence: They saw the right hand of Silvertip slowly convey the cigarette to his lips. They saw the end of the cigarette turn red with fire; they saw it lowered, and they saw the lips of Silvertip part a little, with rippling tides of white smoke drawn inward, disappearing, and with exhalation they saw the cloud of smoke blown with careful aim straight into the face of the sheriff.

Silvertip rode a great chestnut sallion called Parade: He passed the bottom of the valley, and Parade started through the trees, weaving suddenly to this side and then to that, for Parade knew perfectly well that branches which he could easily clear himself might nevertheless sweep his master out of the saddle, and when Silver was on his back, the man was a part of the horse. One nervous system seemed adequate for them both. When they were well up the slope of the mountain, he halted. He dismounted and whispered for a moment into the ears of the great horse. Parade would stand quietly now, straining his ears to hear from his master even the faintest and most distant whistle. And if there were the sound of footfalls coming towards him through the woods, Parade could tell perfectly if the steps of his master were among the noises. Otherwise he would shift and give ground and hide himself with all the cunning of some great jungle beast.

Here now are a few scenes of Silvertip in action: Silver, rising as a cat rises from a long vigil beside a rat hole, stepped from behind the patch of brush to the rear of the trees. He was there as Scotty turned to pick up the shotgun. Instead he got Silver's fist against his chin and dropped in a heap.

"The public ain't welcome behind the bar," growled Pudge.

"Never make exceptions?" asked Silver.

"I don't make no exceptions," said Pudge slowly. Silver dropped his left hand lightly to the edge of the bar, and his right hand with a slight gesture picked a Colt from beneath his coat. There were four extra inches on the long barrel of that gun, and yet it was a feather in the practiced grip of Silver.

Here is a description of Silver as most people saw him: He was big, with a deep, pleasant, quiet tone of voice. His age was between twenty-five and thirty-five. He had a large head, a big brown handsome face. Heavy, capable shoulders gave him the look of a boxer from the waist up and like a runner from the hips down, lean as those of some desert wolf. Above his temples there were two queer little spots of gray hair that looked almost like a pair of horns beginning to grow from his head. There were visible scars on his face where bullets had hit the flesh or drilled through it. Knives had also done their share. He was a survivor of many danger trails, a terror to gunfighters when they crossed him. One man remarked after seeing him up close: "I looked into the face and eyes of an eagle who preyed on hawks only."

The magazine to feature this remarkable individual was Street & Smith's *Western Story*. The author: Max Brand (Frederick Faust). No compilation of western characters would be written without including him. Author John Dinan wrote: "Truly, Faust was king of the western pulp genre."

FLASH STEELE

Wild West Stories and Complete Novel Magazine was published monthly by Teck Publications, Inc., Springfield, Mass. Cost: 10 cents. It was edited by Frederick Gardener. The character we are concerned with here is FLASH STEELE. The author of the stories was Laurence A. Keating. He wrote a blood-filled, gunsmoke saga-like series of stories, and most definitely had a way with words. Here is a rather descriptive passage: It was dusk in the foothills of the sprawling, somber Capitan mountains. The evening star shone like a tiny diamond high in the slate-blue sky streaked orange and yellow and shot with red in a field of colors around the sinking sun. The two riders halted their horses, exchanged rueful, almost discouraging looks through the half-light, and slowly, wearily dismounted.

But now let's get to the hero. "He had no appetite in him for blood-letting that was unnecessary." Such was the attitude of Flash Steele, Special Ranger. He was six feet tall, compact, one hundred and seventy pounds, with wide-shoulders, a leather-tanned face, firm jaw, blue-gray eyes, tow-colored hair. He was one of those roll-your-own cigarette smokers: He lighted his cigarette and inhaled thoughtfully, letting the smoke dribble from nostrils and mouth simultaneously in the characteristic way he had. He rode a horse named Spot, and like other heroes, talked to it a lot of the time. He wore a heavy rubber-butted Colt .45. He wore no uniform or badge while working undercover. He reported only to the governor of the state. The only authority he carried was a letter which served to identify him as a ranger. The letter was inscribed on a piece of onionskin paper and read as follows: To Whom It May Concern: Steele is invested with authority as a special state Ranger, accountable only to me. (Signed: Jim Maridale, Governor.) The letter was destroyed now and then and had to be replaced. In the July, 1936 issue, "Shoot It Out," it now reads: To Whom It May Concern: Bearer, known as Flash Steele, is entitled to prompt and full cooperation at any time from any law officer within the borders of this state. Citizens are urged to assist Steele to the full extent of their ability. Steele is invested with authority as a special state Ranger, accountable solely to me."

Steele kept the letter concealed in a blank cartridge, the fourth bullet from the buckle on his gun belt. The following conversation took place regarding the above: "You claim it's all Steele carries?"

"Sure. Otherwise he's just a floating cow-waddy and nothing more. Who'd believe that young feller with yalla hair and hardly a line in his face? Without that letter, Steele ain't got any more power than a dead monkey."

Here is a segment taken from the November 1935 issue and a story titled "The Devil's Stepson." He swept out his gun. His other hand struck the carbine barrel sideways. The weapon vomited flame across the mane of the roan horse. Steele's Colt exploded as he was leaving the saddle on the far side from the bandit. And as Flash straightened, the fellow's carbine blasted a slug that whipped the sombrero from the ranger's head with a force that snapped his head back. Steele shot once, twice. The tough started a cry that thinned away in anguish. Carbine spilling from his hands, he reeled drunkenly, both hands clasped to his chest. Flash crouched behind the barricade of both horses, the smoking gun in his fist. (He also carried a pocket knife in the pocket of his corduroy trousers. It came in mighty handy now and then.)

In "Killer Range," December of 1935, Steele almost overpowered his adversary but not quite: With all the spring of his slim six-foot body he rose to the footboard, pivoted and drove at Flick with the speed of an ocelot. Steele landed half atop the man and his weapon, half off the rooftop. It was desperate gamble he took, challenging death itself. But his jerk flipped the shotgun from Fleck's grasp. His left fist whizzed at that long oval countenance faintly seen under the floppy brim of the sombrero. But his blow missed. Fleck came at Steele from one side. His arm swept down and the metal-bound butt of a six-gun thudded fully on the Ranger's skull.

One of Steele's closest calls with the grim reaper came in "Shoot It Out," when he was almost hanged: Fighting unconsciousness, he felt himself thrown roughly on a horse. His wrists were firmly tied. There was a noose around his neck, the line running up and over a branch to drop slanting on the saddle horn of Spot. "Make it sudden so he won't holler," a voice said. "I don't want him gagged. It pops their eyes out and makes their faces purple. Well, you tough Ranger, this is your last case." (Naturally Flash got out of that particular tough spot.)

Usually when he finally solved the problem at hand, his body battered and bruised, bleeding from his wounds, he'd just smile and say: "I reckon when I'm shipshape again there'll be orders. Orders to go somewhere, look into somethin'. Trouble, more or less, I reckon. And when those orders come I'll be set, 'cause a feller always wonders what there is over the next hill."

(On a previous page is a reproduction of the October, 1935 cover. The Contents page reads as follows: RUSTLER'S TRAP: Flash Steele, Special Ranger, comes to Kiowa Valley, where two life-long friends are feuding over horse stealing. Flash is blamed by one for all the trouble, but by swift thinking and a lightning draw, Flash shows up the real rustlers.) The story is number 122.

SONNY TABOR

The magazine: *Wild West Weekly*. The author: Ward M. Stevens. The character was Sonny Tabor. One marshal said about him: "I don't care what they say, outlaw or not, devil or an angel, that Kid is plumb full of vinegar and hell smoke!"

Once Ruth Belcher told me: "I like the way he could ride a horse and spin a rope. He even gave the bad guys a fair chance, didn't really want to kill them. I liked his pinto, his beautiful silver saddle and bit chains of silver, his bright colorful Indian-design blankets—his Colt .45's—the way he dressed in checkered shirt, leather chaps, light Stetson. In spite of being called Arizona's number one outlaw, he wanted to keep his record straight. So finally he got a pardon and became a Ranger." He worked under cover as an outlaw. Lester Belcher told about how somewhere along the way Sonny had a girl named Rita.

Let's find out more about him: For instance, did you know he was another one of those hombres who talked to his horse? That he—when doing some deep thinking—often chewed the end of a match? He did not smoke. He usually rode alone.

Sonny was twenty years old, with a boyish face, always smiling, with frank blue eyes and a clean-cut mouth. There was a bullet scar on one cheek. He had always been called "Sonny." There was a certain alertness about him that attracted attention. But he was a cautious man, knowing that out there was many a bullet with his name on it. He took no chances. He once said: "I got letters after my name, too. M.C."

"What's that stand for?"

"Master of Colts."

He could speak Spanish and indeed had a reputation; could shoot as quickly as the bat of any eye. His usual description was as follows:

He wore a vest over a white-blue checkered shirt, brown batwing chaps, a battered Stetson, dusty high-heeled boots. About his slim hips hung a cartridge belt and holsters with two blue-steel Colt .45's. He also had a Winchester rifle.

The first horse he rode was named Chief. It was killed. He then acquired a speedy, powerful, desert-bred pinto called Paint. At age fourteen Sonny was forced to kill a man in a saloon where he shined shoes for a living. His folks were dead, so he drifted around from one place to another. The killing, however, forced him to take to the owlhoot trail. He was to become one of the most feared desperados in all the southwest. It seemed as time passed Sonny would spend a lot of time in some frontier jail, get wounded, and recover. He was a real thorn in the side of the law from Yuma to El Paso. Eventually, while on the prod, he was cornered by a sheriff's posse and almost killed, being wounded in the neck, chest, and leg. A woman, Ma Stewart, nursed him back to health and eventually aided in his escape from jail.

A typical conversation between lawmen might go something like this: "Who is this outlaw you're after?"

"A man known as Sonny Tabor."

"Is he alone?"

"He's a lone wolf, yes. He's a dangerous man. A killer. He's accounted for ten men."

Once Sonny escaped from jail by taking the place of a "corpse" in a wooden coffin, an experience he didn't particularly relish. Another time he was almost hung: They lifted him to the fatal saddle and the deputy adjusted the rope. If he must die, he would meet the end bravely. He had lived as cleanly and honestly as the border country would let him, and he had no regrets. "Let 'er rip!" was the shout. Sonny was hoping that, when the fearful shock came, the jerk would break his neck. He didn't lose consciousness when the terrific yank tore him free from the saddle. He felt his throat close and his head was forced over to the right side. Then, he heard a voice shout, as if from a great distance: "Cut him down, boys!" He was on the ground, the noose was loosened, and he could breathe again.

Here are some action sequences:

(1) The movement of his hands was a blur with streaking flame at the end of it. The crash of the explosion was like the peal of thunder. There was a big blue-steel .45 in each of Sonny's brown fists, and from the muzzle of one of them a twist of smoke curled skyward.

(2) "Reach for it, Sheriff, or somethin' will be smoking around here besides seegars!" The sheriff's right hand moved just a trifle towards the handle of his .45. But he must have seen the quick and dangerous glint in the outlaw's eyes, for he quickly changed his mind and shoved his hands aloft.

(3) Marshal Fargo's gnarled and corded right hand swerved down toward his hip with astonishing speed. "Hands up!" Tabor's voice cracked almost immediately after. Then came the sullen roar of a .45, accompanied by a darting tongue of lightning, for Fargo hadn't obeyed the command. So swiftly had Tabor's twin Colts been snapped from their holsers that nobody caught the motion. It was the work of a magician.

Mr. Harry Steeger
This photograph was presented to the author with the following words:
"For Nick Carr–Pulpster extraordinaire. All best wishes."
(Taken in New York City by Whitestone Photo.)

TEXAS RANGERS

ACTION WESTERN STORIES

ALL STORIES COMPLETE

THE LONE WOLF RIDES

A COMPLETE FULL-LENGTH NOVEL FEATURING THE WEST'S MOST FAMOUS OUTLAW-HUNTERS IN ACTION

BIG CASH PRIZES FOR WESTERN MOVIE FANS

Texas Rangers was published bi-monthly by Better Publications, Inc., N.L. Pines, President. Cost: ten cents. According to pulpologist Albert Tonik, Jim Hatfield, the hero of the novels, was the pulp character who had the second most stories written about him. (The Shadow rated first.) The adventures were written under the house-name of Jackson Cole, in reality a variety of authors. Among them, A. Leslie Scott, Tom Curry, C. William Harrison, Lee E. Wells, Dean Owen, Walker A. Tompkins, D.B. Newton, Clark Gray, Joseph Chadwick, Peter Germano, Roe Richmond, Lin Searles. Most of the covers of the magazine depicted an action scene of one sort or another.

The man of action was JIM HATFIELD, better known as "The Lone Wolf." He was a person who never believed in advertising his presence until advertising was expedient. He was also a man who professed a love of good music and could play a piano and guitar. He also danced with the grace that comes from perfect coordination of mind and body. Once following a dance Hatfield smiled at his little dance partner: "Hasta luego, Senorita," he told her. "Be seeing yuh." The big-eyed girl gazed wistfully after his tall form as it vanished through the swinging doors into the night. "The kind that's always leaving," she murmured to herself.

When Hatfield arrived on the scene in the first story, the Sheriff complained: "Here I got a fust-class cattle war on my hands, and they send me one Ranger."

"Well," Hatfield drawled, "yuh only got one war, ain't yuh?"

Upon reaching the local hotel for the night, Hatfield signed the register and went to his room. The hotel man mused over the signature written in a firm, legible hand. "Cowboy, maybe, but he ain't always been one. Feller don't learn to write like that twiddlin' a grass rope. I betcha that jigger's got learnin'." The hotel man was partly right. Jim Hatfield was the son of a well-to-do cattleman. He had two years of college before unfortunate speculation coupled with two lean years of drought and blizzard had cost the elder Hatfield his ranch. Worry eventually caused his death. His education interrrupted, Jim went back to cowpunching, then eventually drifted into the Rangers. In time he would establish a most unique reputation. One thing that would help him a great deal was the fact that he had studied geology while in college.

At Ranger headquarters the company captain, "lean, tall, gray of eye and tight of mouth," was in conversation with a lieutenant named Bayles. The captain, it was said, "would charge Hell with a bucket of water." HIs name was William McDowell, gnarled as an ancient oak. He stood about six feet. Kept behind a desk now because of his age and "some other problems associated with it," this grim, grizzled, crusty ranger had ridden many a danger trail over the red-earth plains of central Texas, the chaparral jungles of the Nueces, and the lush semi-tropical Gulf Coast. "This blasted rheumatism," he growled. "If it weren't for that, I'd be in the saddle right now."

Captain "Roaring Bill" McDowell, head man at the Austin headquarters, had a temper for sure. "I saw a sawbones recently," he went on, "and he told me I'd live to see a hundred and twenty if I quit lettin' my temper get the best of me." (Well, he thought philosophically, a man has to grow old sometime.) But McDowell ruled with an iron hand and a velvet glove. His impelling power was felt throughout the state, wherever men bucked law and order. A big man, broad-shouldered, a six-footer, with a frosty face, white hair, and blue eyes.

"Anyhow," McDowell continued, "all hell's busted loose in one particular section and we got tuh send somebody to put things right. You know they ain't no law west of the Pecos."

"Who do you want to send?"

"How about the Lone Wolf?"

"Yuh mean the young feller Brooks sent over?"

"Uh-huh. He's got brains, and guts. I'm told he likes to work by hisself. That's how come he got his nickname. When he's with a troop he's just another good ranger, but when he's off alone he's a terror. Ain't never failed to outhink and outfight any smart jigger he's been sent after."

"Sounds good. I like men who want to go in single-handed." Some minutes later when Jim Hatfield came into the office it was his eyes that held the captain's gaze: They called to mind eyes of men who had walked through the smoke-misted West with hearts unafraid; in whose presence other men were wont to speak softly and move their hands with care. In terse sentences he outlined the problem. "They's yore orders. Once yore outa this office yuh use yore own judgment 'bout things."

"Yes, sah." Hatfield asked no questions. He turned and walked out of the office. The captain grunted: "That jigger might as well work alone. He shore ain't no conversation help to the folks around him." (Later on McDowell would say of Hatfield that "he was the greatest Ranger to have joined the organization since the legendary Jack Hays in bygone years." His statement was borne out by other old-timers.)

Another time when Hatfield reported in for a new assignment, McDowell said; "How soon can you leave?" The Ranger paused a moment, then replied: "I'd like a couple of hours sleep first." McDowell growled right back, "Take four. If a Ranger ever slept more'n four hours at a time, the owlhoots'd plumb take over Texas."

So Hatfield left the small office and returned to the barracks. As he sat on his bunk with a cigarette, the barracks "was suddenly filled with the shadows of men who were gone forever. Comrades of many long trails and vicious combats, dead and buried in lonely graves, scattered from the Sabine River to the Palo Duro Canyon of the Red River. Hatfield saluted them all. (The Austin headquarters had a parade ground, administrative building, commissary where all of the supplies were drawn, stables, a cook shack, bunkhouse, and barracks.)

Hatfield rode a sorrel named Goldy. In perfect harmony, it could very easily be believed they were on a footing of friendship rather than one of mount and rider. The impression was heightened when Hatfield talked to the horse, for Goldy seemed to listen and understand. The horse was trained to allow no hand other than Hatfield's to touch him.

Jim Hatfield was pictured as follows: More than six feet tall, wide of shoulders, slim of waist, he rode with the easy, careful pose of a man who had spent his life in the saddle. Heavy Colts hung in carefully worked and oiled hand-made holsters. He lounged easily in the saddle and his green eyes were sunny. He held the rank of lieutenant in due time after proving himself. He rode out on some of the toughest cases.

Here is another description: His face was deeply tanned, and his mouth firm and rather wise, his nose straight. He had a broad, thoughtful forehead and thick, crisp black hair. His eyes were very long, darkly lashed and of a peculiar gray-green. They were the type of eyes associated with sudden death.

From the novel "Panhandle Guns," December 1943, we have this portrait: The huge rugged Ranger was ready for duty. He took off his Stetson to smooth the black hair on his handsome head. The strap had left lines in the firm flesh of the strong jaw, which was unprotected by any hirsute growth, for he was smooth-shaven. Long muscles rippled under his clothing, an indication of the tremendous power of the man. At his waist, which tapered down from broad shoulders, rode a belt supporting smooth-stocked Colts. In action Hatfield was Hades on wheels, swift as legerdemain, deadly as a striking tiger. And in anger, those mild gray-green eyes could turn to the dark green bleakness of an Arctic sea. He wore no badge openly, but kept his silver star snugged in a secret pocket under his shirt. He was indeed a man for all seasons.

Hatfield carried the scars of battle on his body, and one of his closest brushes with death must surely have come about in "Gunman Play the Long Odds," September 1956. He was ambushed and shot. It happened this way: The fire of the setting sun was dying behind the hills. The flat prairie lay in darkness. Below, the ahallow pool under the cutbank reflected the bright aquamarine streak of sky. Hatfield took two steps along the bank, searching for a way down to that shallow pool. An owl gave its thin, lonely sound again and now something warned Jim Hatfield, a sense of danger as intangible and yet as definite as a passing shadow. But the shot came before he moved. He felt the smash of the rifle slug in his chest, knocking him sideward. He fell off the cutbank into a well of darkness. A small man stood over the lip of the cutbank and gazed down at the sprawled figure lying with his right arm and shoulder in the still pool. The ambusher slid down the bank and crouched beside Hatfield. As he turned him over he noticed the slight rise and fall of the Ranger's chest. His eyes explored the blood-rimmed bullet hole at the edge of the shirt pocket. "He's dying," the voice said. "Fifteen miles from nowhere. Without a horse—without a gun. He'll be dead before morning. He's got one chance in million. Not even the devil himself can buck those odds."

But fortunately Hatfield survived and, given five weeks to recover, he was ready to once more ride the trail and hunt down the ones responsible. But then he was accustomed to riding and fighting singlehanded against odds when need be; he was physically well-fitted for such missions. This giant who we know stood six feet four was built in a manner that combined grace and speed with power and stamina. He handled himself with easy assurance, calm and controlled in every fluid motion, unquestionably a person to be reckoned with. His look of bleak, grim toughness was relieved only when he smiled.

From "The Lone Wolf Rides," October 1936, is this segment: "Hatfield covered the remaining ten feet like a charging wolf. His boot toe caught the fallen man's wrist and sent the gun spinning from his hand. Then the Ranger's iron grip fastened on his collar and jerked him erect. A voice cold as frost-covered steel cut at the stranger, the muzzle of a big Colt jammed against his ribs. "Yuh figure yuh done lived too long, feller?" he asked.

Here is another: Suddenly the Ranger, watching in the mirror, saw fierce black eyes centered on his back. The squat man's slit of a mouth pitched a word at his companions. They stiffened, following the direction of his glance with narrow eyes. Three pairs of hands swept down. Jim Hatfield left the bar like a coiled spring. He slewed sideward, whirled and leaped all in a single flashing move. His intention was to throw the three gunmen off balance and also to get away from the crowded bar before lead began to fly. His guns come out almost at the same instant. The three killers began shooting and the big room fairly exploded with the roar of blazing Colts. Hatfield, weaving, ducking, hands steady as rocks, answered them shot for shot. Down went the squat leader, drilled dead center. One of his companions suddenly rose on tiptoe and shrieked. The shriek chopped off short as he coughed blood down his shirtfront. Then he crumpled like an old sack. The third man dived frantically for the outside. Jim blasted the swinging doors to pieces after him. The whole thing hadn't taken ten seconds. The saloon was in a panic-stricken uproar. Women were screaming hysterically, men cursing and shouting.

Gunsmoke on the Rio

Featuring Jim Hatfield, Ranger!

The Thudding Hoofs of a Mysterious Night Rider Pound Out an Ominous Message of Bitter Range War——While Murderous Rustlers Hurl a Defi at Ranger Justice!

The Lone Wolf came to his feet catlike, a gun in each hand. (Page 41)

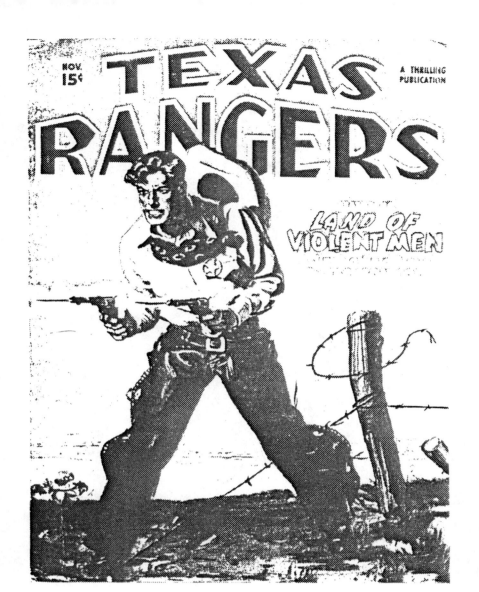

NOV. 15¢

TEXAS RANGERS

A THRILLING PUBLICATION

LAND OF VIOLENT MEN

"What yuh mean by throwin' lead at my riders?" he bellowed (Page 29)

The Lone Wolf Rides

Senorita Scorpion

Action Stories, published by Fiction House, Inc., featured the above-named lady. The author who apparently did the bulk of the stories was Les Savage, Jr. Emmett McDonald also contributed. Among the stories we read were "The Return of Senorita Scorpion," "The Curse of Montezuma," and "Senorita Scorpion." As we were writing this article another crossed our desk, "Sting of the Scorpion." They were quite enough to convince me she belonged with her male counterparts here in this book. Most of the covers featured the senorita, who was indeed well endowed with the necessary attributes. Very slim looking, she was pleasing to the eye. As one particular cover told us: "Her kiss was flame. Her gun was doom." One contents page ran as follows: "Lovely, flame-topped Senorita Scorpion and Marshal Tony Dexter were cuttin' the same sign—almost. She was gunnin' for the coyote that knifed her kid brother—and he was grimly on her trail, carrying Colt-vengeance for a murderess!" (She had two brothers, one called Johnny, the other Natividad.)

With an introduction like that, wouldn't you be tempted to pick up an issue of the magazine?

So just who was this woman the Mexicans called Senorita Scorpion? She's a devil, they all said, lightning with a knife, or a whip, or a gun. Her real name was Elgera Douglas. She rode a palomino horse named La Rubia (The Blood).

She rode like fury and carried a big Army Colt with black rubber grips, along with a Winchester rifle. She was indeed a woman who could most certainly take care of herself in almost any situation. To demonstrate this, here is just one incident: The woman waited until he was directly beneath the rock, then rose to her hands and knees and jumped with a wild, husky sound. They hit the ground with a jarring thud. The man lay underneath, taking most of the shock. The woman rose to straddle him, laying the barrel of her gun against the side of his head.

Here is another action sequence: Elgera threw herself forward, grabbing the man by the legs. They rolled in the grass. The girl fought savagely, biting, kicking. She came on top of him and rammed a vicious knee into his stomach. He choked and doubled up, trying to jab upward with the big knife. She caught his wrists. He tried to jerk the knife from between them before his final weight descended upon her. He came down heavily, his body stiffening suddenly. She struggled from beneath him, seeing that he had plunged the knife into his own body by rolling on it.

We have this description of Senorita Scorpion: She had an obliquely formed face, golden hair, blue eyes, and was tall. There was something wild in the arch of her eyebrows, a tempestuosness in the piquant curve of her pouting lower lip. She was made much taller by the spike heels of her boots. Her legs, long and slim, were encased in Charro pants.

There is also this view of one hell-for-leather woman: "He bent forward in the chair, glittering little eyes licking up the turn of Scorpion's lithe legs and the curve of her breast under the ducking jacket."

The tall slim roundness of her body was accentuated by the tight yellow blouse caught in a red sash and her clinging leggins of buckskin with bright flowers sewn down the seams. Behind the narrow black mask her eyes were blue, and her long blonde hair cascaded around, shmmering in the sunlight, stunning and unbelievable against the high colors of her face.

Illustrated by
C. A. MURPHY

The male interest in the story we looked at a couple of times was Marshal Tony Dexter. There were others also. Dexter had a strong, roughly-hewn face, black eyes. The nose was high, almost Indian in shape. His jaw was strong and angular, smooth as copper. He was very broad through the shoulders. He rode an Appaloosa and carried a six-gun. At this time it seemed that Elgera was head lady of the Circle S Ranch located in the Lone Star State. She led a most complicated life and to tell her full story would take up more pages. Because of this I suggest the reader try to locate the August 1985 issue of *Echoes Magazine*. Inside you will find an article by pulpologist Robert Sampslon titled: "About Senorita Scorpion." This is as in-depth as one can get. You will encounter all of those associated with her, such as the Sheriff of Brewster Conty, Johnny Hager; Father Douglas; Ignacio Avarillo, a Mexican mining engineer; plus those villains who pursued her.

We couldn't help but wonder how Senorita Scorpion might "stack up" against those females found in some of the other pulp magazines. For instance, from *Spicy Western Stories* (June 1941 issue) an epic titled "Girl in the Saddle," by John Pearson, serves the purpose very well: There was something magnificent about the way she held herself. She was the largest woman Rattlesnake had ever seen. Her hair was raven black, her mouth a sullen gap in the smoke-begrimed circle of her face. She kept her shoulders well back, her breasts jutting proudly, half covered. The rags of a skirt fluttered about her full hips, scarcely concealing the muscled litheness of her thighs, the sturdiness of her legs. The breeze whipped the tatters about her legs, her breasts trembled and swayed at each determined step.

Here is one more from the same story: Ruby usually woke up in midafternoon. This morning she awakened nearly four hours before her regular time. Ruby was ageless. Her body was svelte and sleek and well kept. Her breasts were those of young woman, firm and arrogant; her sleek hips and finely chiseled thighs were a mad sculptor's dream.

Now from "One Man's Death," by John Phillips: One hand went up, tore at the neck of her dress and ripped it almost to her waist, partially exposing the soft roundness of her breasts.

From an issue of *10 Story Western Magazine* is the following paragraph found in a story written by Morgan Lewis titled "Prodigal's Gunsmoke Lesson": Her brown hair curled crisply about her smooth brow and her brown eyes were dusted with little gold flakes. Her nose was straight and slightly upturned at the tip, and her red mouth held a full, generous curve.

Rangeland Romances, October 1935, had the following from a story by Oliver King titled "Wild and Sweet": His eyes swept her from head to foot, taking in the threadbare calico dress, shapeless and scrupulously clean, which hung from her so that no curve of her body showed—if she had any, apart from the delicate swelling of her bosom which somehow made itself felt, bud-like, under the worn cotton.

Thrilling Ranch Stories had one called "Ghost Bullets," by Ryerson Johnson.

The gal involved was Evelyn Beal. The story ending goes like this: "Breeze lifted her head, his fingers brushing over her hair, kissed her tenderly. Then he kissed her again, long and hard."

The Pecos Kid Western series had women involved, of course. Naturally the Pecos Kid in all of his wandering met all kinds. They could be from across the tracks in Dodge City, Kansas or some of the more sophisticated ladies along the vast frontier. One such female happened to be named Joneyjo Lee. She was dark, slim in the waist with full hips and bosom. She wore a dress of amber satin that brushed the floor. It was without ruffles or folderols. Her skin under the oil lamps had a tawny cast. She reminded Pecos of a jungle cat. Her teeth were as white as bits of shell. Her arms went around his neck. She sat in his lap. She took his head in both hands and pulled it against her bosom. "I think you're the man for me."

"But are you the woman for me?"

"I'm plenty o' woman," and smiling, she drew a little switchblade dagger. "After I kiss yo', I'll slit your throat." She leaned back. Her hair was in jet ringlets that hung down towards the floor. Her eyes were closed, waiting for him to kiss her.

LEN SIRINGO

The magazine: *Star Western,* a Popular Publication. The author: Ryerson Johnson.

Star Western had some very high standards, set by editor Rogers Terrill for the authors to follow. He wanted (and usually got) "stories with meaty plots which are the outgrowth of colorful and honest characterizations. The drama in our stories is not obtained by a blast of six-gun slugs in every paragraph. The western atmosphere we desire is developed naturally through characterization, colorful descriptive action and plot situations peculiar to the west. We especially seek stories that have an epic sweep, where the results of action will change the history of that community and where there is something more vital at stake than the personal problems of the hero and heroine."

As another writer put it: "They (referring to the breed of men like Siringo) were born in an era of violent change the likes of which the human race may never see again. Skill with a gun, skill in killing, gave each one tremendous power."

Probably author August Lenninger said it best in a *Writer's Digest* article, "Six of a Chain," with these words: "The American West was one of the most glamorous frontiers the world ever knew."

So it was that Ryerson Johnson gave *Star Western* just what it wanted—LEN SIRINGO—and other characters as well. But first of all get one thing straight—this particular hero was one hombre who called no man "Boss." He could be characterized in a number of different ways: An avenger who came stealthily as the wind, who struck as ruthlessly as that same blast whipping down from the high ranges. A lone wolf, eccentric, free lance range detective; a phantom gunner; freedom's gunman. One of the most talked about men in the West, and the most seldom seen! His actual physical description wasn't all that easy to come by, but here is how we saw him: He had a long, gangling frame, and looked as though he were put together in hodgepodge fashion. His mouth was a slash under a great hawk's beak of a nose; hair, thick, black on a high forehead; eyes gleaming with a kind of dry burning. He possessed a deep, resonant voice. His favorite weapon, an ivory-handled Colt .45 Peacemaker. His reputation had spread as far away as England, where they had "heard about his deeds of derringdo."

He did work now and then "in loose cooperation with the Cattlemen's Association." He was a rather sinister gent who seemed always absent when he was right there on the job. One time when his name came up, this exchange took place:

"Len Siringo? Who's he?"

"Where you been all your life? I didn't know the deserts were deep enough to bury the reputation of Siringo," the other hombre replied.

Another waddy said of him: "You come here like you do everywhere, sizin' up things in secret. You're here and nobody knows about it."

But it took a lot of nerve to even think about sending for him, because many letters writers got a bullet in the back for their trouble, along with a permanent place in the nearest boot hill. One such letter might read as follows: Mister Siringo, we've all heard how you hate gun-rule and injustice worse'n rattlesnakes. And how you range around puttin' a lead finish to same. Mister Siringo, there's more gun-rule and injustice to the square mile here in Los Flores valley than anywhere outside of hell. Wherever you are lone ranging, drop everything for God sake and get here quick.

Siringo was pretty handy with his Colt. It turned into a deadly weapon in his expert hand. It seemed he was able to draw with the speed of a striking rattlesnake, and at a hundred feet could plate a Mexican copper coin with lead six times out of six. Once Siringo had caught a hombre dead on the end of his gun muzzle. The man threw up his hands and so Len held his fire. "You're rather take a chance on a rope than shootin' it out with me?"

"I figure," came the quick response, "a man's got a slight more chance on the end of a hang rope than on facin' you through gunsmoke."

Here is a seququence from a May 1941 story called "Red Hell Hits Gila Crossings" that speaks for itself: "Sounds like a job for Len Siringo. Why don't somebody send for him?"

"Send for him? If Siringo got one out of a hundred letters that was ever sent to him it'd be a miracle now, wouldn't it? That gunner for the law goes cruisin' up and down over a million miles of frontier. He's like the wind—you hear it in the trees, but where does it go? Same way with Siringo. You're always hearin' about how he'd come on somewhere and gun-pried somebody out of trouble, but I never met nobody that ever saw that crusin' range-detective actual, did you?"

Siringo in his role as "freedom's gunhawk" had once been a printer's devil in his younger days; he also was hired by the railroad to be a troubleshooter just one step ahead of the construction gangs. The way things always worked was like this: He'd arrive, but never as Siringo. Instead he would be in disguise as a lightning-rod salesman, a tinker, a professor, a doctor, engineer, undertaker, rainmaker—what have you. He'd come with names like Doc Soak, Gimpy, the claimjumper, Dishwasher Dan, a chuckwagon cook. In one epic he drove a wagon with the words: Dr. Higgenbothem's Original-Double-Distilled Fireside Remedy—on the sides. This character was a "red mustached individual with eyes that looked out fiercely from beneath bushy red brows."

Siringo was by no means unaware of the female sex. One happened to be Ruth Sewell, daughter of a printer named Zeb. She was "the kind of girl cowboys would ride forty miles just to hold her in their arms at a schoolhouse dance." In the print shop she said to Siringo: "This isn't your fight." He replied: "I took the job, ma'am. And if have to clean up a town before I can print a paper, well, I reckon I'll just have to clean up the town." She leaned closer to him. There was a gleam in her eyes and her cheeks were flushed. Siringo had cruised around enough to recognize hero-worship when he saw it. She was so young, so lovely. With unbelievable gentleness the famous man said, "It's only dazzlement, child. It ain't me, close up, that you love. It's Len Siringo, mystery gunwolf, tamin' a town somewhere far off."

(You can read all about in it "Len Siringo Prints with Gun-Type," November 1939 issue, when he rode to the aid of the *Greasewood Sentinel*.)

Some others might recall Siringo this way: Although he looked awkward, his rather disjointed stride covered distance at an astonishing rate. His voice was soft, deep-throated, pleasant, yet oddly stirring. He had a thin, homely mouth, long neck, heavy eyebrows. Usually when on the prowl "the skin was pulled tightly on thin cheek bones."

From another story is this episode: The driver of the buckboard was tall and lanky. He wore a high-crowned black hat, a long sack coat, tight pants, and—what was more important in Deep Wells—a holstered six-gun. A black string tie drooped from his standup collar. His face was long and sad, with eyes narrowed and lips tight on an unlighted stogie that jutted straight out.

He looked like a funeral about to happen. The load carried on the buckboard—long narrow boxes, some painted white, some red, some blue, piled high and lashed together with rope. "I'm Ben Graves," the stranger announced, talking around his stogie in a hollow, oddly resounding voice. "Ben Graves—Boothill Benny to my pards.

Undertaker by trade. I hear tell this is likely territory for one, so here I am, boys—" His long slim fingers at the end of his long arm waved out towards the buckboard—"ready to set up business and wait on customers. First come, first served."

"You don't mean," someone demanded, "them red, white, and blue boxes is—"

"—coffins," Ben Graves finished in a voice like the crack of doom. Just a few paragraphs later big trouble breaks out and Ben Graves faces a showdown. He watched as one individual sized him up. What that person saw he sure didn't like: The man's long body was bending slowly, twisting into a sinister crouch. His slack coat would be no impediment to his reach whenever he decided to go for his gun. The man took notice that the walnut butt showed sign of hard usage, and that the holster had been oiled and hand-kneaded for smooth drawing. "If you're askin' for a ride in one of your own boxes, it's all right with me," the man said. "Fair enough," the undertaker acknowledged. "I always like to grant a doomed man his last request."

Here is another demonstration: Chewed-Ear said, "You better drop your gun." Doctor Higgenbothem (Len in disguise) didn't drop it. But he turned away. With a swiveling motion close to his side, he arched his six-gun barrel and put one shot into the Idaho Twins. The slug plowed into the Idaho Twins holster where it was fastened to his belt and left both belt and holster hanging by shredded leather. The Idaho Twins jerked his hand away from the gun, and Doctor Higgenbothem swiveled back on Chewed-Ear Claxton. The move had been so breathntakingly fast that Chewed-Ear hadn't been able to take advantage of it. "Drop it," Doctor Higgenbothem said. "I'm countin' three." He started counting and at the second count Claxton dropped his gun.

One thing for sure—Len Siringo hated gun-bullies and range hogs, and had dedicated his life to a close-out fight with the forces of injustice which clamp over any town and newly created land. He rode the frontier righting wrongs with the cunning of his brain and the force of his trigger finger.

WALT SLADE

Thrilling Western featured another well established Texas Ranger by the name of WALT SLADE. The author: Bradford Scott, actually A. Leslie Scott. This leading man was tall, well over six feet, about two hundred pounds, with wide shoulders, a deep chest, lean, sinewy waist. Arms long, ending in slender, muscular hands. Eyes a reckless pale gray, the color of a glacier lake under a stormy sky. Hair black. The face, deeply tanned, had a hawk-like profile above a powerful jaw and chin. He had a deep, commanding, rich sounding tone of voice, a wide mouth, grin-quirked at the corners. He played a guitar, carried in a waterproof case across his broad shoulders. He had a very fine singing voice, a golden baritone-bass.

His usual attire: bibless overalls, blue shirt, a neckerchief looped at his sinewy throat, scuffed half-boots, and a broad brimmed hat. Around the waist, double cartridge belts with cut-out holsters holding plain black-butted Colt .45's. He also had a high-powered rifle, a long-range Winchester, the weapon built to Slade's own specifications.

He kept his ranger badge in a "cunningly concealed secret pocket in his broad leather belt." Once removed, he'd toss it on a table where everyone could see it—a gleaming silver star set on a silver circle—the feared and honored badge of the Texas Rangers. Then after a few moments Slade would slip the silver star back out of sight. Usually it was the last thing some outlaw who had been gunned down by Slade ever saw before he expired and was carted off to the nearest boot hill.

Slade's boss was the Commander of the Border Battalion of the Texas Rangers, Captain JIM McNELTY. Slade rode a great black horse called Shadow. When he spoke to the animal, Shadow usually gave an explosive snort that undoubtedly meant whole-hearted agreement. Shadow was a one-man horse, who allowed nobody to touch him without his master's sanction. Slade rode "with the easy grace of a lifetime in the saddle, swaying lithely to the movement of the horse."

Slade had graduated from college with a degree in Engineering. His father died largely as a result of financial reverses that caused the loss of the family ranch. Slade had previously worked with the Texas Rangers during his summer vacations and finally decided to sign up with them even though he received offers from engineering firms for a lot more money. It was a choice he never once regretted.

As Slade began to work undercover as a Ranger, he built up a dual reputation. He became known as EL HALCON—The Hawk, "of dubious repute," with killings to his credit—"an owlhoot too smart to get caught, but who'd someday end up in boot hill." As El Halcon, avenues of information were open to him that otherwise might have remained closed. El Halcon—the good—the just—friend of the lowly and all who suffered injustice and oppression. "May El Dios ever guard him," his close friend, Estevan, a Yaqui-Mexican knife man said. Estevan was a tall, lean man with a dark, savage face and glittering black eyes If you happened to talk to any of the peons of the river villages about El Halcon, they'd tell you that when Slade's black brows "drew slightly together it was a sure sign the big man was doing some pretty serious thinking." Those same Mexicans might tell you that when Slade did take time out to do some singing, his voice was as sweet as the wind whispering through the pines, as deep and powerful as the white water roaring in mountain gorges. They'd also say that Slade had the ability to size up a situation in split seconds.

As the top undercover ace of the Rangers, Slade, who understood and spoke Spanish, roamed the trails across Texas. He was one of those roll-your-own smokers, usually managing each cigarette with the slim fingers of his left hand. His hearing was especially acute, picking up sounds nobody else could detect.

He could handle guns with the best of them: The great horse shot forward. At the same instant Slade's hands flashed up and down. Both his guns let loose with a rattling crash as he sent a storm of lead screeching and hissing over the heads of the men.

From the novel "White Gold," June 1947, is this sequence: "Hold it! That's far enough!" the voice rang out as musical as the call of a silver bugle, but edged with authority. Slade walked easily forward several paces, and halted. His eyes were the color of frosted steel. The thumbs of his slim, terrible hands were hooked over his double cartridge belts and directly above the outflaring butts of his heavy guns. Abruptly those hands flashed down and up in a move too swift for the eyes to follow. There was a spurt of flame, the crash of a shot. One of the masked riders clutched at his blood-spouting shoulder. The gun he had slipped from under his black robe fell from his paralyzed right hand. His companion jerked spasmodically, as if in sympathetic reaction to his agony. Then they froze in grotesque, strained positions before the menace of the two black muzzles, one wisping smoke, that yawned hungrily towards them.

Here is a short paragraph from "Walt Slade Rides a Trail," November 1950: Craig Talo, with a scream of fury, went for his gun. He was lightning-fast, but Slade drew and shot him between his blazing eyes before he could clear leather.

Another interesting episode: "Blast yuh!" the man sputtered. "If yuh didn't have the drop on me, I'd show yuh!" Slade's hand moved with bewildering speed. Then, the big gun back in its holster, he lounged carelessly in the saddle and regarded the other man with cold, reckless eyes. "Haven't got the drop on yuh now," he remarked softly.

"Wrong. Yuh got the drop on us even with yore iron holstered. I know a quick-draw man when I see one." The man's eyes took in the tall form of the Ranger, more than six feet in height, lounging with the careless grace of a lifetime in the saddle. He studied Slade's straight, long, black-lashed gray eyes. He saw the broad shoulders, the wide mouth, the prominent hawk nose. The bronzed hands of the Ranger rested on the saddle horn.

Once Slade had a close-call with the grim reaper: El Halcon was a light sleeper at all times, and tired though he was, when a slight sound out of the ordinary came into his room it aroused him instantly. Abruptly he was awake and aware that the sound continued—a slight, sibilant sound like the hissing of a large snake. He sat up in bed, glancing about, and uttered a sharp exclamation. On the floor, just below the window sill, bloomed a flower of fire that crept steadily toward the bed, throwing off a spurtle of tiny sparks. An acrid smell stung his nostrils. Slade bounded from his bed, instantly recognizing that pungent whiff of smoke for what it was. He groped frantically along the floor until his hand encountered a couple of greasy cylinders bound together with wire. He seized the dynamite sticks and started to throw them out the window, but realized that the tree branches grazing the window ledge were apt to rebound the deadly thing back into the room. There was no time to fumble for a knife, and he dared not risk jerking the fuse from the cap clamped to the dynamite. Setting his teeth to the tough fiber covering of the fuse, as near as possible, he chewed frantically. The fuse resisted stubbornly, and ever the sputtering bloom of the fire crept closer. Slade redoubled his efforts, tearing at the resisting fibers that gave so slowly. He felt the fuse part, a stream of sparks searing his mouth, and for a terrible instant he feared he was too late. But even as he stiffened in anticipation of the explosion that would tear him to bits, the severed end of the fuse dropped to the floor and sputtered out with a final baffled hiss. El Halcon straightened up, holding the dynamite in his one hand, and mopping his streaming face with the other. "And that was close," he muttered. "Another shake of the coyote's tail and they would have had to take up what was left of me with a blotter." He closed the window before lying down again. Fumbling for the "makin's" from his pocket, he rolled and lighted a cigarette carefully, shielding the tiny flame of the match in cupped hands.

Often when some job was finished they offered to cut Slade in on his share: "Don't need much in Ranger work," he said. "Besides I haven't got time for it. Captain Jim will have another little chore lined up for me by the time I get back to Headquarters. You fellers ride into town and tell the sheriff what happened. I don't want to be here when he comes around askin' questions. If it got generally known I'm with the Rangers, my value to the outfit would be considerably lessened. I'll be trailin' my rope tomorrow, early."

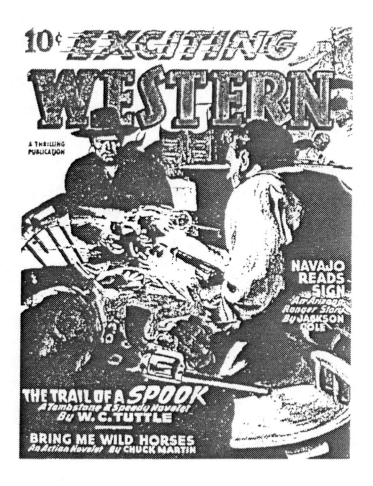

TOMBSTONE JONES

SPEEDY SMITH

TOMBSTONE and SPEEDY

The magazine: *Exciting Western.* The author: W.C. Tuttle. The characters: A couple of range detectives named Tombstone and Speedy. Last names were Jones and Smith.

"Murder is almost always fatal." With an imperturbable outlook like that, just how can Speedy Smith miss becoming a top intellectual? It wasn't easy, believe me. On the other hand, when somebody brought up the fact that William Shakespeare had been dead about two, maybe even three hundred years, Tombstone Jones said: "Is it that long? Time shore does fly."

Now outside of being absolutely negligent, dumb, improvident, and two of the biggest liars in the entire state, those two could—and did—blunder into the solution of every case detailed them by the secretary of the Cattlemen's Association, believe it or not. The fact they even worked now and then for the Association was some sort of a miracle in itself.

The secretary, Jim Keston, knew both men were absolutely unversed in detective work, yet they had a way of cleaning up some pretty tough cases. Much to Keaton's surprise, Tombstone and Speedy never once filed a report. They weren't exactly the best-dressed hombres around either. Usually they wore overalls, nondescript shirts, well-worn high-heeled boots, battered old hats, and they always needed haircuts and shaves. Both of them were inveterate gamblers. The minute any money came into their hands, both headed right for the nearest gambling house. They came out flat broke every time.

Once, however, the two did get five hundred bucks reward apiece. So what do they do? They buy champagne, of course, at twelve bucks a bottle. Let's take a look first at Jones: He couldn't read or write. Although he had no education he had a big imagination. He was almost seven feet tall in his boots and sombrero, lean as a greyhound, long of face, with sad-looking eyes. A lock of natural-colored hair bisected his forehead. He never could find a bed made long enough for him to sleep in. Smith on the other hand was five foot seven inches tall, built otherwise along the same lines as his friend. He was bowlegged, and weighed about one hundred and ten pounds. Once he had even tried to grow a mustache, but really never had much luck. Both could shoot, but their gun belts and holsters and guns were very plain and also well worn.

Let's take a look at the two in action. First example is from "The Ghost of Angel Springs," March 1951: WHAP! The man forgot he was still in reaching distance of Tombstone's long right arm and that hard fist hit right on the nose. Speedy was diving for the other man, hitting him low and hard, and the man went off his feet, sprawled across the hot stove. It was all done in split seconds, and then they were diving for the doorway, with Speedy knocking the lamp off the table as they went past. The man with the ropes didn't have a chance when they crashed into him, leaving him in a tangle of ropes.

From "Shotgun Evidence," November 1950: Then they heard Tombstone say quietly, "You come on time, my friends." They saw the moonlight glint on the barrels of the shotgun as the man drew it from the bush, and a split second later the gun flamed—both barrels—at point-blank range. The smashing reports had barely bounced back from the wall when Speedy, coming from somewhere out of the brush, hit the man with a flying tackle. Even Speedy's hundred pounds, going at top speed, was not to be denied, and he took the man almost into the well.

It seems that Tombstone had a very tender nose, as we learn in this short paragraph: Tombstone swung half around, dived ahead, reaching with both hands. He got hit again, but this time it was only a glancing blow, and a fraction of a second later his hands grasped a man's arm. The man hit him in the nose, which was already very tender, and then Tombstone really went to work. The only time he missed a punch was when the man wasn't upright. Then Tombstone fell upon him and went to work again.

2 FULL BOOK-LENGTH WESTERN NOVELS
W. C. TUTTLE — G. W. BARRINGTON — WES FARGO

JANUARY
BIG-BOOK WESTERN
MAGAZINE

W. C. TUTTLE

Novelette

WARWHOOP WILSON WHOOPS!

Full Book-Sized Novel
GUN STAMPEDE
By WES FARGO

Big Novel
SHERIFF OF TWIN CREEK *By* G. W. BARRINGTON

WARWHOOP WILSON

The author: W.C. Tuttle. The magazine: *Big-Book Western*. WARWHOOP WILSON was the deputy sheriff of a frontier town called Bearpaw. He had the job of keeping law and order when the real lawdog was away on business. Wilson wasn't a real big man and not even handsome, but there was a quiet confidence about him that lent a strange charm to his bow-legged appearance. He was only fair with a gun—he was not "gun-fast" in the gunman's sense of the word. He carried a walnut-handled Colt in a holster affixed to a dark-leather cartridge belt. He usually rode a lean, long-legged gray horse named Sandy. (For once we are not informed if he had any conversations with Sandy or not. He didn't in any of those yarns we read.) He was one of those roll-your-own smokers and did have a particular pasttime—playing, of all things, a jew's harp. (This is a small lyre-shaped instrument which, when placed between the teeth, gave tones from a bent metal tongue struck by the fingers.) This musical (?) habit of Wilson's usually didn't sit too well around Bearpaw.

Warwhoop's friend, Windy Lane, a freckle-faced puncher for the Rafter C Ranch, complained many times, "'What's the matter?' You playin' that hell-harp an' you ask 'what's the matter?' Ain't nobody shot you for playin' that thing inside the town limits yet?"

"Not yet, Windy. I been tryin' to remember how that second verse that you taught me went, but I forgot." Winday said: "Don't. I'm young yet and ain't seen all of the world I want to see. An' if Bearpaw finds out I taught yuh any of yore songs, they'll lynch me for sure."

When Warwhoop burst into song it was much like a musical wail   Before taking on the deputy's job, Warwhoop had been a cowpuncher on the Rafter C Ranch.

Warwhoop Wilson in a scene from "Jew's-Harps and Six-Guns," appearing in the September 1935 issue of *Big-Book Western*.

Dusty Trail

Steve Reese

Hank Ball

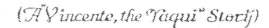

The Canyon
of
Frozen Horror

by Wilson Campbell

VINCENTE, THE YAQUI

"I am a Yaqui," he spoke. "I can go away from here without disturbing a leaf. They think to make fools of us. But only for so long will they succeed. Sooner or later, Vincente will find him out. You are a fool. But let me warn you. If you torture me, be sure you cause my death, for as long as I live, your life will be worth nothing!"

Thus spoke a man with a high-boned face, wide shoulders, and long, powerful arms. They called him Vincente, the Yaqui, "a magnificent hunk of Indian manhood." He had deep black, dark eyes, sometimes described as "hooded eyes," and a broad back, corded with lithe muscle. He was a person who seldom revealed his true feelings. He was an excellent tracker. As one man had said: "I ain't seen a trail he couldn't follow, and he's followed some I couldn't see." He carried as his main weapon a long-bladed knife and rode an even-tempered sorrel horse named Tortilla.

Early on his life was saved by one Alf Chase, son of the owner of the Z B Ranch. As Vincente told him: "You once saved my life. Now I am always your shadow. I am only beginning to pay the debt I owe you."

Alf Chase was young, with clear gray eyes, a pleasant mouth, trim face, heavy level brows. He had big, stern hands. His horse was a black steed named Ink.

Here Vincente is seen in action: Vincente's long-bladed knife flashed wickedly in the sun as the Indian sprang forward, swift as light. The guard never knew what struck him. Folding up like a collapsed balloon, he pitched forward and lay still. But this action, quick as it had been, awakened the relief sentry. Instantly, on seeing the half-naked Yaqui drawing his dagger from the dead man's body, he lifted his gun to fire. The movement did not escape the Indian. Quick as a flash he straightened up, the knife flying from his hand, cutting a glittering arc through the air. With a gasp of pained surprise, the second guard crumpled as the thin steel blade quivered in his chest.

(2) On Vincente came, his sweat-covered torso glinting golden in the sun. On, on, on— then his brown arm flashed backwards, darted forward again, and a silver streak sped from his sure hand. Again his dagger found its mark. Luke Stern pitched on his face, spitting crimson flecks and cursing horribly, and then was still.

(The above illustration is from a story in *Wild West Weekly,* located for us by Lester Belcher from his vast collection. The author was Wilson Campbell.)

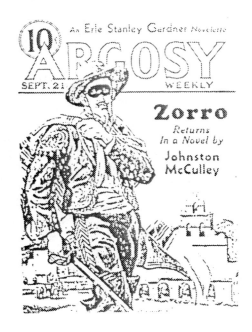

The magazine: *All-Story Weekly*. The dates: 9 August—6 September, 1919. The title: "The Curse of Capistrano." It was in five parts. The author: Johnston McCulley. The character: ZORRO. He was and still is a pulp hero many of us will remember for as long as we live. Zorro's second appearance was in *Argosy-All Story Weekly*, 6 May—10 June, 1922, a six-part epic titled "The Further Adventures of Zorro."

From a checklist furnished by Edwin Murray of Durham, North Carolina, we know this masked avenger's appearances were as follows: *Argosy* six more times; *Cavalier Classics*, twice, July and September of 1940; *West* a total of 58 times; *Max Brand Western*, just once, May of 1945; *Short Stories*, once, April of 1959; *The Best of Argosy Bicentennial Issue*, once, 1976.

Edwin Murray has some comments about the author: "It is a shame he is not known for Zorro the way ERB is for Tarzan. He was a prolific writer who began doing period pieces for the pulps because history was always his main interest. The Zorro stories are a continuity freak's nightmare. One way the pulp Zorro

is different from the television Zorro is in his sign. The TV character carved a "Z" sign on his opponent's coat. The pulp Zorro did it on the guy's face with three separate sword strokes. Another favorite sport of the pulp Zorro was horse-whipping the villains."

Here are some observations from pulpologist Robert Sampson about Zorro: "The wicked are punished by whipping or by carving a "Z" into their foreheads or cheeks. Some few he ran through, for he is a faultless genius with a rapier. At the end of the first novel, the secret identity is revealed and he wins the beautiful girl. She later dies. His identity as Zorro is conveniently forgotten."

According to pulpologist Will Murray, "Zorro is a major American hero of much the same caliber as Superman, Tarzan, and the Lone Ranger."

Now from *Argosy*, 21 September 1935, in a story called "Mysterious Don Miguel," we have this: "The gambling ceased abruptly. All in the room whirled to face him. Before them, standing against the wall with his arms folded across his breast, was a man who wore neither cloak nor hat. His blouse of black silk was open at the throat. He had a blade at his side, and a dagger in his girdle, and a pistol in his sash. Over his face was a closely fitting mask of black, which concealed his features effectually."

From the pages of *West*, a Thrilling Publication, we find a different Zorro emerging. Now astride a black steed, he rides over the hills and back trails with pistol, sword, and whip—to punish those who mistreat the helpless.

The scene is the hacienda at dusk, just before the evening meal. Don Diego is with his father, the dignified Don Alejandro, Fray Felipe, and Bernardo. "You will ride the black horse as usual?" asks his father. "I have instructed Bernardo to have everything ready." Don Diego nods. "Good fortune ride with you, my son. Every time Zorro rides I worry and pray he will return safely. You are the only one left in our family to follow me when I am laid to rest. Moreover, if you were caught you would be hanged, and our estates confiscated."

From another adventure, "Zorro's Twin Perils," May of 1946, in *West,* we find a most descriptive passage: "The costume was ready. Also his weapons. Quickly Don Diego put on the costume over his outer clothing, put on the enveloping black mask, belted on the blade, and thrust a loaded pistol into his sash. He coiled the long, stinging whip he sometimes used and straightened his shoulders."

The true identity of Zorro was of course DON DIEGO VEGA, son of Don Alejandro Vega, owner of a vast ranch property near San Gabriel. Diego always seemed to avoid any physical exercise, and spent much of his time reading the words of poets. "A mixture of milksop and popenjay" other young caballeros said of him. But naturally all of this was a pose. Three men knew his secret from the beginning: Don Alejandro; Fray Felipe, a Franciscan padre attached to the little chapel in Reina de Los Angeles and Diego's confessor;

and Bernado, a huge mute who acted as Diego's body servant. To Diego, Bernardo was a man in a million, loyal to the death, a staunch defender, a man who could and would fight at his master's side. Twice Bernardo had saved Diego's life—once when a rattlesnake had struck him in the fields. Bernardo has slashed the wound and drawn the venom from it with his lips. Again, when Diego had fallen from the back of a stumbling horse into the path of a wave of stampeding cattle, Bernardo had ridden to his rescue and pulled him to safety.

Over the years naturally there were others who knew his secret role. But the one picture most of them had of Diego was observing him walking the plaza in Reina de Los Angeles, holding a scented handkerchief to his nostrils, his eyes half closed. Slowly he would move to one side of the plaza where the dust would blow away from him instead of upon him.

One of the more interesting characters in the series was Sergeant Manuel Garcia. He would preside over the Reina de Los Angeles barracks during any time his superior was absent. It seems he ran "to brawn more than brains, was a jovial fellow at times and a stern disciplinarian at other times." The responsibility of attending to the military matters in the district during the absence of his captain weighed heavily upon him.

On the other hand, according to Will Murray, "Captain of the local soldiers was a very hazardous job with Zorro around. One man after another took the post only to be scarred and run out by Zorro. Captain Carlos Ortega was a major figure in *West,* lasting through the first fourteen issues before leaving."

Another man to serve as commandante was Captain Juan Ruelas, sent from Monterey to take command of the entire district. (See "Zorro's Fight for Life," *West,* July of 1951. Ruelas was known as an extremist in brutality. He was a tall, lean man of middle age, with a hawk-life nose, glittering black eyes, a mass of black hair. On his left cheek a scar ran from the corner of his eye to the tip of his chin. His uniform was ornate, heavy with gold braid, and the hilt of his rapier was studded with jewels. It was his arrogance and extreme brutality that earned Ruelas the wrath and vengeance of Zorro. His downfall came in this manner: Zorro stopped at a line of whipping posts in the center of the plaza. "Captain," he said, "I'm going to give you some of the medicine with which you have dosed others. You will be found in the morning dressed only in a nightshirt that has been cut with a lash across the back. Everyone will know that Zorro took you from your own barracks and brought you to this." He untied the captain's wrists, one at a time, forced each arm upward its full length, lashed it to the crossbar with the leather thongs. Then Zorro got his whip from the pommel of his saddle. He lifted the whip and swished it through the air. The very first blow cut the skin and stained the nightshirt with blood. Zorro lashed again and again, ten lashes in all. Ruelas slumped against the whipping post. The whip was coiled and fastened to the pommel again. Zorro took his blade from the scabbard, and Ruelas's body flinched and sagged even more as the tip of the blade cut between his shoulder blades. Then Zorro mounted his horse and rode slowly out of the plaza. Left behind was the captain, and between his shoulder blades a letter "Z" had been carved.

In our eyes, and I suspect yours also, we have always pictured this masked rider astride a black steed riding cautiously down some hidden trail. He has become a part of the night itself. The moon passes from beneath a cloud and for a few moments we see, coiled around the pommel of his saddle, that long black whip which could give such terrible punishment to wrongdoers.

It was Don Diego who remarked: "It is said that a man who treads carefully walks a long distance."

RIDERS OF THE GUNSMOKE TRAIL

As we indicated to the reader earlier, when it comes to those western pulp characters, only the surface has been touched and probed in this book.

Wild West Weekly, for instance, featured more individuals over the years than one can imagine. We can only hope that some of your favorites have been included. Now you will meet a few more, from that magazine and others, in a sort of "thumb-nail" portrait. Each was tall in the saddle.

THE BORDER EAGLE

His real name was TRIGGER TRENTON, a former U.S. Deputy Marshal (who still carried his badge). Aged about 32, he rode a leggy roan called Flatfoot. His weapons were two bone-handled Colt .45's. The author was Philip F. Deere.

BLACKY SOLONE

A former Texas Ranger who kept his badge in a pocket of the left leg of his chaps, he rode a big black horse and was another of those roll-your-own smokers. Solone was a giant of a man, over six feet tall, lithe, with a huge tapering body, deep chest, a yard-wide at the shoulders, with a swarthy face. His gun was a double-action, walnut-stocked Colt .45. His usual attire: a beaded buckskin vest, gray shirt, dark pants, boots, spurs, hat.

The author: James P. Webb.

RAWHIDE RUNYAN

He ran the Diamond Double R Ranch. He had a cook known as Limpy Watson. His ramrod was Slow Joe Hill, a big, powerful, wide-shouldered man who "could kill a man with a swipe of his arm." A reformed outlaw, Hill had a powerful temper. Runyan rode a black horse called Shadow. His ranch was located in Rainbow Valley, Arizona. He was five feet nine inches tall, one hundred and fifty pounds of "whalebone and rawhide," with gray eyes, a tanned face, and wide shoulders. Age: twenty-four. His usual weapon was a Colt .45 Peacemaker. Once a hombre said to him: "You ain't the law." And Runyan replied: "That's right, I'm not. But this old Colt in my hand is all the law I need." Author: Chuck Martin.

ROWDY LANG

Another so-called outlaw who hated killers and never had robbed anybody. There was a large reward for his capture. He was another of those roll-your-own smokers and always kept a sack of tobacco in his vest pocket. He rode a tall bay horse named Star. He was tall and lean, with a muscular frame and had slate-gray eyes in a copper-brown face. He carried a Colt .45 in a worn holster, tied at the bottom through two small holes in the right wing of his chaps. He also kept a snub-nosed .38 in a shoulder holster under his left arm. He kept a full supply of ammunition in his saddle bags at all times. He had a strange habit of wearing a glove on the left hand, right hand bare. The author: James P. Webb.

TOMMY ROCKFORD

He was a captain in the United States Border Patrol, with headquarters down in El Paso, Texas. His immediate superior was Captain Sam Lodge, who referred to Rockford as "his star rider of the Rio Grande Division." Rockford had quit work on his father's ranch to first become a railroad detective and then later a federal officer. Thirty-two years old, he stood about six foot two, lean-looking, with blue eyes in a face bronzed by exposure to the Texas sun. He wore batwing chaps, a blue workshirt, kangaroo-leather boots, and a gray Stetson. His guns were twin gold-plated .45's holstered at his flanks. He rode a Kentucky thoroughbred roan horse. His father was Jeff Rockford, owner of the Star W ranch in the Texas Panhandle. The old man, now 68, was blind in one eye due to an opaque cataract covering the iris. He had a goatee and pure white hair. As a matter of fact, he resembled Buffalo Bill Cody quite a bit. The author was Walter A. Tompkins. He once wrote Lester Belcher and explained just how he started the series: He said he happened to be at a railroad station and noticed a package adddressed to Rockford, Illinois. The idea "hit him for Tommy Rockford, Railroad Detective."

SILVER JACK STEELE

He was young, gray-eyed, dark-haired, with a single lock of silvery white which had given him his nickname and reputation among the Wyoming Territory outlaws. His blazing Colt .45 sent many an owlhoot to his final rest in some lonely boot hill. Here is a quick look from one of the stories: With a yell, Silver Jack leaped to his feet. He hurled the hay fork towards the shotgun. As he threw, he drew his Colt and drove the bullet through the side of the barn. The heavy slug tore through the soft pine boards like a hot knife cutting butter.

RISKY McKEE

His nickname came from a bad habit he seemed to have—accepting wild bets against the outlaw fraternity when the game called for action and bullets. Risky had a ranch of his own in New Mexico and raised cutting horses. He was a young hombre with a sun-tanned face, who wore a tan denim hat and checkered shirt, and carried a Colt .45. He rode a roan pony. His partner was a lanky, toothless, baldheaded character called SUFFERIN' JOE. Now Joe's garb consisted of foxed buckskins and moccasins. He constantly complained to Risky of his numerous imaginary ailments, and had been fired from every decent job he had held. "My stomach is gettin' more painful every second," Joe told Risky. "You know darned well that I must have drunk a mess of frog eggs in that water at the last spring we passed. I most likely have got frog poison or somethin' sproutin' right inside my gullet."

"That story is as old as Dan Moody's hound dog," Risky replied. "I'm tired of listening to your latest bellyache. Fork your bronc and let's ride."

Here is a short segment from "Bullet Poison," January 31, 1942 issue: Risky loosened the .45 six-gun in the holster tied down to the thigh of his leather chaps. "Pard," he told Sufferin' Joe, "you ride in from the south side. I'll ride in from the north. That's just a precaution against us both being salivated at the same time." He turned the sorrel pony off the road to enter Blisterville. He slowed the horse to a walk as he drew near a hditching rail in front of a saloon. The barroom door opened, and several hombres in straw sombreror moved outside. "Buenas dies, Senor McKee," one called out. Risky's nerves tightened. "Howdy, Miguel. Nice weather, ain't it?'

"Very nice weather, Senor McKee. But soon eet get mucho hot."

"Glad to know that. I'll find a shady spot and wait for it."

THE OKLAHOMA KID

JACK REESE was his name, an outlaw much better known as The Oklahoma Kid. There was a sizeable chunk of reward money offered for him—dead or alive. He was always very cautious about letting other people get too close to him. Deputy Ed Sparks had reward posters all over the country. His usual hideout was in a remote stretch of the Arizona badlands. He had one real and loyal friend in Sheriff Al Tapper, a gaunt, grizzled man with gray eyes and a weathered face.

Reese was a small, wiry individual with a hard-bitten face, thin mouth, black brows and hair of the same color, with beady eyes close to a long, lopsided nose. His garb was usually buckskin trousers and a pale-yellow shirt. He wore matched six-shooters with age-yellowed ivory grips. He rode a chunky, blaze-faced horse called Shorty.

Here we see the Oklahoma Kid in action: (1) The Kid moved swiftly along the wall, guns in his slim hands. His features went granite hard, and his slim thumbs hooked back knurling gun hammers and let them fall. (2) The Oklahoma Kid had been standing with hands raised to shoulder level, his weight balanced on the balls of his feet. As Cotter barged up, the Kid's wiry body suddenly swiveled half around and his right fist shot out in a looping blow that had his spinning weight behind it. Cotter was too slow to jump clear. The Kid's fist landed on the point of his jaw. Cotter went down, hard, his six-shooter clattering on the stony earth.

From "Boothill for Paradise," June 27, 1942, another segment: The Oklahoma Kid pivoted to face new danger. He felt the breath of a bullet against his cheek and heard the deathly whisper of still another before he could complete his turn and bring his own weapon to bear on Linkler. The man was scurrying towards a bend up the wash, firing twin guns in a furious burst as he retreated. The Kid's guns rolled out stuttering replies, and his bitter eyes watched Linkler stumble, hobble on a few paces, then pitch silently down under the hammering impact of two well-placed bullets. Slowly the Kid stood erect, aware that a bullet had struck him along the right side some time during the battle. In the camp, excited men were yelling, and Tom Donnelly was moaning and trying to get onto his feet. "Think it over before you start any more trouble," the Kid warned. Author of the series was Lee Bond.

HUNGRY and RUSTY

The author: Sam H. Nickle, who wrote a fast-paced, full-of-action account of the trials and tribulations of two Texas Rangers by the names of HUNGRY HAWKINS and RUSTY BOLIVAR. They worked under the watchful eyes of a crusty oldtimer named Captain Roberts.

"Lobo Masquerade," August 29, 1942, has this: "Hungry was the fastest gunman in the entire ranger service. Little Rusty was plenty fast, but his lanky partner's flashing draw and deadly accuracy was still more uncanny!"

Whoa! Maybe I better tell you a bit more about them. Hungry Hawkins was a tall, lanky, lantern-jawed fellow with a homely face. He had one bad habit: "He pulled a battered plug of strong tobacco from his pocket. After he tapped it against the saddlehorn to shake off any clinging sand, he wiped it on his sleeve and thoughtfully gnawed off a huge chunk." He was an accomplished accordion player. His usual weapons were Colt .45's which sagged the cartridge-filled belt down low on his hip.

Rusty Bolivar, on the other hand, was a little, bow-legged, blue-eyed, freckle-faced individual. He wore his Colts on criss-crossed cartridge belts. He was also one of those roll-your-own smokers and he played a jew's-harp. Both men rode well-trained horses.

Here is one more scene from the story mentioned above: The blustering stranger's beefy face mottled with killing fury, and he dropped his hairy hands as if to stab for the pair of white-handled .45's. But as Hungry's carbine muzzle jerked toward him he saw the deadly greenish glint in the lanky ranger's slitted eyes, he caught himself. Little Rusty had not left the scene, and now his hands smacked his Colt butts in a blurring draw at the first hint of gunplay. Face twisted in a fighting scowl and his blue eyes flint-hard, he stood with both hands on his weapons.

A lot of the time both men were sent out on assignment with orders to keep after the killers until they were run down, no matter where the trail led or how long it took. In "War Drums on Loma Grande," October 31, 1942, both men were getting ready for action: Hungry's homely face hardened. He frowned. Jerking his guns from his holsters, he hurriedly examined them to make sure they had not been fouled by blowing sand. When he and Rusty had looked at their short-barreled carbines and made certain they were fully loaded, they slid their rifles back into the brush-scarred scabbards beneath their right legs and touched their mounts with spurs. "Watch closely now," drawled Hungry grimly, his slitted eyes riveted on that faint plume of smoke. "If it is them hombres an' they see us comin', they'll most likely take to the brush and try downin' us from there. Be ready to hit the ground and go down on yore horse's side if the shootin' starts."

JOHNNY FORTY-FIVE

His real name was Johnny Socrates Forty-Five. He was "a brash, salty, little United States Deputy Marshal." Here we have his description as written by author Andrew A. Griffin in the story called "Where Sheriffs Fear to Tread," from the April 18, 1942 issue: The sheriff's eyes flickered, then stayed open. To the brisk tune of jingling spurs and clicking boot heels, a grinning young half-pint was swinging cockily along the plank sidewalk. There was certainly nothing of the lawman about him. His flannel shirt was faded to no particular color, and his hard-leather chaps were so badly worn that they would have been scorned by many a thirty-a-month cowhand. The Stetson tipped jauntily over one eye had seen better days. This deputy didn't bother to display a badge. His manner was so carefree that not even the sheriff's shrewd eyes took note of the business-like way he carried his guns. They were heavy-caliber matching Colt .45's, single-action model, each tucked in a well-oiled holster thonged low on his leg. The jutting handles of the guns were scoured smooth by many a draw, the blue finish having been worn away from the steel back straps. Johnny rode a wiry, quick-stepping buckskin horse. He would often make up rhymes in reply to questions. He absently rolled a cigarette with a quick motion of his left hand, tossed it away, and laced one just as rapidly with his right. Johnny explained in rhyme:

"It's just a little thing I do
To exercise the trigger finger;
If I should get the roomatiz,
My soul on earth not long would linger."

His associate was another marshal named George Krumm, a big man, fat, with a well-rounded face, close-cropped brown mustache, and a double chin. He would often brag: "Sure you ain't heard of me? I'm Iron Man Krumm, Fearless Krumm, The Terror of Evildoers." He carried around well over two hundred pounds. In "Ruin To Renegades," January 31, 1942, Krumm was hanged: The fat man, his feet about a foot from the ground, was turning lazily at the end of a rope, his head to one side, his tongue out between his teeth. But luckily Johnny was on hand to save his life. When Krumm finally came back to his senses, he said: "They killed you too, Johnny? What world are we in?"

"You're far from dead," laughed Johnny. "They strangled you instead of breakin' your thick neck."

From the story mentioned above, here is a part of the second chapter: "I don't like sleepin' out in the open like we're goin' to have to do." Krumm shivered a little. By way of reply, Johnny rolled—and flipped away unlighted—another of his tanpaper cigarettes. His fat pard scowled at him with irritation. "I wish to blazes you'd quit that foolery, Johnny. Bein' as you don't smoke, I'd think you'd get tired of twistin' up them brain dusters thataway." Krumm had just finished the contents of a whiskey flask a few miles back—he claimed that he had felt a cold coming on—and Johnny reminded him of it, while explaining his quirly-rolling:

"It's fine for trigger fingers, George.
And it keeps my gun hands spry;
I think it beats yore recipe
Of soakin' 'em in rye."

"Now you know I never drink except for my cough," Krumm protested. "And that danged fool po'try of yours will drive me—Hey! What th'—"

A buzzard with a dead snake in its talons had risen from a nearby ridge and Johnny had whipped out one of his six-guns from its holster and fired. It didn't seem possible that he could have taken aim, for the Colt flashed and roared the instant that it left the leather. The carrion bird, however, plummeted earthward in a cloud of flying feathers. It was really a miraculous shot, but Johnny seemed to think nothing of it. "That was purty fair shootin', Johnny, but nothin' like the kind I've done," Krumm said softly. "I remember once down in Texas when I had the same target—bird with snake. Only it was a live rattler. First I shot the snake outn his claws, second shot I killed the bird, third shot I cut the head off the snake afore it hit the ground. After that they called me Deadshot Krumm down thataway."

"And up here you're Halfshot Krumm, thanks to the whiskey you just guzzled," Johnny Forty-Five grinned.

THE WHITE WOLF

Author: Hal Dunning. The White Wolf was in reality one JIM–TWIN ALLEN, a raw-boned outlaw who had "a legion of Texas Rangers after him." There were bounty posters spread from the panhandle to California. White Wolf gave allegiance to no man and put his trust only in his guns and his speed, along with two gray cow ponies, Princess and Gray Combat. He was small, but whipcord lean, 120 pounds, standing five feet five inches tall. His eyes were flecked with yellow and were wolf slanted. His face and small hands were sun-bronzed. His usual garb was that of a saddletramp, consisting partly of cactus-scarred bullhide chaps and a gray shirt. Twin Colt .45's rested low in thong-tied holsters. In one story, "Hot-Lead Homecoming," October 31, 1942, he decided to pay a visit back to his home range, and in particular the Bar L Bar Ranch, Arizona Territory. That sprawling, sage-dotted range encompassed the only good memories he knew. There were four people he just had to see: the ranch owner, Ian Macpherson and his wife; a cowpoke named Toothpick Jarrick, and a blue-eyed, curvesome, flaxen-haired girl, Snippets Macpherson, age twenty. Her love for him was the one good, clean force in his life and this prevented him from becoming the cold, ruthless killer wolf some men claimed him to be. But it was a love he could never claim as long as he was on the dodge, riding the owlhoot trail.

So naturally that homecoming was marked by a special display of fireworks by Mr. Colt: "You can take your choice of beatin' my draw or waitin' for the law to put you under arrest. I ain't particular one way or the other," spoke the White Wolf. He watched as the lawyer halted. The saddlebags slipped from Calhoun's shoulder. Instinctively his reflexes had jerked the lawyer's gun up, so that the bore of his Colt was on a line with the hard-bitten outlaw framed in the doorway. For the space of ten heartbeats, the tableau held. The odds were that both men, pulling triggers simultaneously at point-blank range, would go to their deaths together. Aware that he faced one of the most deadly gun aces in Arizona Territory, the lobo attorney likewise knew that surrender meant arrest, and arrest would bring inevitable doom via the hang-rope. Calhoun made his choice. His knuckles went white outside the trigger guard of his gun, and that tiny detail telegraphed his decision to the outlaw waiting in the doorway. Flame ripped from the White Wolf's poised guns, a shaved instant before the Colt roared and bucked in Calhoun's fist. Firing alternately from his two weapons, Allen hurled himself to one side as Calhoun's first bullet clipped his sleeve and drew a warm wash of blood down his forearm. A two-gun agent of destruction, the White Wolf continued firing until Judge Calhoun, dead on his feet but still triggering his Colt at the empty doorway, pitched headlong and thudded face forward onto the rug, which was absorbing the lifeblood from a dozen wounds in the lawyer's frock-coated frame.

KID WOLF

"Where's yore credentials?"

"Heah, sah," he murmured, tapping the butt of his six-guns. (Pretty good credentials, I'd say.) My name's Wolf. Those who like me call me Kid, and those who don't play my game seem to find somethin' fitting in my last name." (Words to ponder indeed.) "I'm just a soldier of misfortune goin' through life trying to do all I can fo' the weak and oppressed. I'll risk mah life fo' those people." He spoke in the soft accent of the old South, yet with a trace of Spanish, a musical drawl. He came from the Lone Star State and rode a fine horse with a spotless hide of snowy white, fittingly named Blizzard. The Kid's saddle was from California and concha-decorated. Nobody could touch Blizzard but Kid Wolf. He was simply a one-man horse. When the Kid wanted to summon Blizzard in a hurry he'd let out a coyote yell—"Yip, yip yipee—ee!" The white stallion recognized his signal and came running to him "like a white snowstorm." He was a white demon in action: Before the Kid a deep arroyo yawned. The walls were steep. A full twenty feet wide, a tremendous leap. The Kid felt Blizzard rising in the air. If the horse failed, death waited on the jagged rocks thirty feet below. But he made the jump. (The Kid was another hombre who often talked to his horse).

Kid Wolf was young, lithe, slim-waisted, with broad shoulders, long light hair, a clean-cut, deeply tanned face, very white teeth, keen blue-gray eyes. He stood tall and very straight. Twin rows of cartridges criss-crossed his waist, and low on each thigh hung a holstered, wooden-handled six-gun. The belts were of carved leather. The Kid would use sandpaper on the wooden handles of the guns to roughen them slightly, remarking, "I wouldn't want to have my hands slip when makin' a draw." He also carried a bowie knife in the collar of his shirt, and this weapon saved his life many times over. Usually he wore fringed buck-skins touched here and there with the gay colors of the Southwest and Mexico, along with a wide sombrero and low-heeled boots with the lone star of Texas in studs of silver. He was good at cards, spoke Spanish like a native. But he was above all a plainsman. He could find water where there was none; discover game where others failed; follow a trail with ease. He simply wasn't a man to fool with: One stride and Kid Wolf had him by the neck. For all the man's weight and in spite of his bulk, the Kid handled him as if he had been a child. An upward jerk dragged him from the chair. The Texan held him by one muscular hand.

Once he was asked to surrender his weapons: "I am an American, sah. I try to do good. What I've done, I've done with these." The Kid tapped his own Colts. "I've twelve lead aces here, sah, and I'm not in the habit of layin' em down."

Here are examples of his skill: (1) The Kid's hand slapped down on his right Colt. A blaze of flame leaped from the region of his hip. Along with the crashing roar of the explosion came a sharp metallic twang. The bullet had neatly clipped away the man's belt buckle. (2) Kid Wolf drew his left-hand Colt so quickly that no man saw the motion. Before they knew it, there was a sudden report that rolled out like thunder—six shots blended into one stuttering explosion. He had emptied his gun in a breath! (3) Kid Wolf's left hand snapped up under the gun and rapped sharply at just the right spot on the wrist that held it. It was a trick blow—one that paralyzed the nerves for a second. (Actually the Kid could draw both weapons with the speed of light.)

The Kid tangled with a saloon owner named Jack Hardy, a flashily dressed gunman-gambler. He wore a fancy-stitched pair of riding boots, a fancy vest, and a short black coat, from under which peeped the butt of a silver-handled .45. But this time it was with fists and not guns: Hardy sent a smashing right hand jab at the Texan's heart. Kid Wolf blocked it, stepped to the outside and lashed the rustler king under the eye. Hardy staggered back against the table, clutching for support. At close range, Kid Wolf smashed at him with both hands, his fists smashing in sharp hooks that landed on both sides of Hardy's jaw. Then, putting all the power of his lean young muscles behind his sledge-like fists, he hit Hardy twice. The first blow stopped Hardy, straightened him up with a jolt and placed him in position for the second one—a righthand uppercut. It landed squarely on the point of Hardy's weak chin. He went hurtling through the door, carried off his feet.

One thing we almost forgot to mention was that Kid Wolf would often sing when he was in the saddle. Here is a song that we liked, from a story titled "A Buckshot Greeting"—

Oh, the cows stampede on the Rio Grande!
The Rio!
The sands do blow, and the winds do wail,
But I want to be where the cactus stands!
And the rattler shakes his ornery tail!

Before we leave Kid Wolf here is one final look as he faced up to another challenge: "Yo' can surrender—and in that case I'll turn yo' over to the nearest law, if it's a thousand miles away. Or yo' can shoot it out with me heah and now. It's up to yo'."

"You want to see my gun?" said Goliday. "I'll show you what's in it!" Like a flash his hairy hand shot downward toward the ivory-handled Colt. The ranchman's hand touched the handle before Kid Wolf even made a move towards his own weapons. Goliday's eager, fear-accelerated fingers chopped the hammer back. The gun slid half out of its holster as he tipped it up. There was a noise in the adobe like a thunderclap. A red pencil of flame sneaked out between the two men. A gun dropped to the hard dirt floor. A round dot had suddenly appeared two inches left of Goliday's breastbone. He dropped heavily to the ground.

Kid Wolf has his own particular philosophy: "I'm just a rollin' stone. I just naturally roll towards trouble. Yuh'll find me where the lead flies thickest."

Blizzard cocked his ears and turned his head to look his master in the eye. Blizzard savvied. He was "in the know."

It was Ruth Belcher who made a study of this character. She once told me: "I like Kid Wolf because he was straightforward and wanted to overcome evil. He fought for the underdog. I think the best story was from a particular December adventure. It told of Christmas time and doing things for the Quakers and the nesters."

The author was Ward M. Stevens.

From the pages of *Wild West Weekly* allow me to turn now to *Western Novels and Short Stories*, a 15-cent magazine. From its pages come The Ramblin' Hombres:

TEX and PECOS

Their real names were Tex LORMER and Pecos SCOTT. Or: Aloysius Algernon Percival Scott, although nobody but Tex ever knew it. In addition to the above title of The Ramblin' Hombres, they were often called "The Inseparables." This was because the two never stayed long in any one place, but together roamed over the vast southwest in in search of adventure. According to the author, James Lassiter, the two "worked together like well-oiled machines."

These two bullet-welded saddle pards were both bronzed and lean-jawed. They dressed pretty much alike in dark wool shirts, bandannas, corduroy trousers, high-heeled boots, spurs, vests, and rolled-brim sombreros. Their wide cartridge belts of yellow leather rested on slim hips. Holsters held single-action .45's.

One ranch foreman remarked: "That pair carries restless guns, slippery holsters, and itchin' trigger-fingers. Thank Gawd there's a heap more good than bad in 'em."

Tex Lormer was a rangy fellow, raw-boned, red-haired, with humorous gray eyes and a tanned weather-beaten face. Pecos Scott, on the other hand, was small, wiry built, dark-complexioned, snub-nosed. He had a wide mouth that tilted upward at the corners, giving his face an expression much like that of a medieval gargoyle. Theirs was a strange attachment, as both were reluctant to show any real display of affection. They covered up by continued insults, but these were always accompanied by understanding grins: "I been wonderin' how I could get rid of you for the past couple of years," Tex said. "You never resisted a temptation in your life," Pecos retorted. "That's just why I've stuck to you, trailin' along to pull you out of the messes them temptations get you into!"

Here is just a part of "Colt Call for Fighting Men," May of 1939: "Hands off, you fellers, this is a private quarrel."

"We're makin' it public!" Tex yelled. The man in the doorway fired, but his aim was bad. Tex's hand flashed down to his holster, came up in one smooth rhythmic movement holding his Colt. The thumb slipped from the hammer, white fire darted from the blue-steel barrel   The man in the doorway sat down suddenly with a broken leg. Pecos had already pulled his gun and downed one of the attacking Mexicans.

The Western Pulp Artist

In an article written for *Unicorn,* Volume 11, Number 2, titled "My Favorite Jungle Stories Covers," I said in part: "The artists, I have been told, carry each of us into lands of fantasy with their paintings."

Just think what the pulps would have been like without their fine covers and great interior art. A horrible thought. Time and time again I've heard these words: "Covers sold the magazines."

True indeed. So this book wouldn't be complete without a chapter devoted to the artist. But first a question: "What is an artist?" Webster tells us: "A person skilled in one of the fine arts."

Norman Saunders

One such individual was Norman Saunders. He was associated with numerous pulp magazines, Popular Publications among them. Although he spoke just a couple of times with Harry Steeger at Popular, he said: "Harry was a busy man. He was, however, very nice to work for and every once in a while he would send word down to the editor or art director when he was pleased with one of my paintings."

Saunders also painted the first cover for a western titled: "The Pecos Kid." He did not sign it, but supposedly has the cover proofs to this very day and is pretty sure the original oil painting is up in the attic of his home. "That was during the time Mike Tilden was an editor at Popular," remarked Saunders. He had this to say about fellow artist Walter M. Baumhofer: "I have admired him for many years—nearly forty-five or more now. I think he was one of the greatest pulp artists that ever existed. He was one of the very first to respect the pulp magazines and his own product to the extent that he always painted from live models. Prior to Walt, the average pulp-cover painter used old scraps and clips from pictures to produce a cover. There were a few exceptions—but very few. Walt had a male model that he employed at a weekly wage for a number of years. It was the magazine *Doc Savage* that gave him the opportunity to turn out a class "A" cover—and he made the most of it. He really hit his stride when Steeger hired him for Popular Publications' western, mystery, and detective covers. He really turned them out—and all of them good, along with a number of really excellent ones."

Saunders himself had a fine background for the pulps. He painted covers also for Dell, Street & Smith, *Ace Magazine,* and others. He most generally did sign his paintings, especially during the Thirties, but not so much in the Forties. The reader has probably seen his covers for *Jungle Stories, Public Enemy,* and *Mystery Adventure.*

He had this to say about *Public Enemy:* "The cover was one of my earliest paintings, and it was really very pulpy. I sold my first pulp cover to Dell about six months before this one. The editor was Wes Peterson and the art director Victor Julius. Vic was a great art director and helped me a great deal. The model was Joseph Birdsal. He modeled for me about six or seven years and had black hair—not blond. Public Enemy was painted in August of 1935, and I received $75.00 for it."

He also did one for *The New Mystery Adventures,* April 1936, to illustrate a story called "Those Without Graves." "I painted it for a publisher named Walt Hubbard," Saunders said. "He was a press agent for AAA and liked Japanese girls and oriental food. I painted quite a number of covers with a morgue as background. They didn't allow photos of morgues in those days, so I had a preacher I knew write a letter of introduction saying I was a student mortician visiting New York City, and to please allow me to go inside and look the place over. I got in and made a flock of pencil sketches from memory the minute I got out. So I had a lot of real information for future use. You would hardly think so, though, looking at this cover in MA." Then he added: "The other day I received a couple of photos from a fan—of two covers—oil paintings I had painted about 1933. I had really forgotten about them, as that's over fifty years ago. He paid one thousand dollars for them, I understand; I received one hundred dollars when I painted them."

(The photograph included in this segment depicts a western scene as artist Saunders planned his first drawing outline for one particular cover.) Saunders has resided in New York City for many years, but recently decided to move to Nebraska.

WALTER M. BAUMHOFER

"The time I spent in the pulps—about ten years—were, I think, the most fun of my whole life," Baumhofer said. "Sure I enjoyed the slicks, particularly enjoyed the money. But I enjoyed the pulps more. When I delivered a painting to Harry Steeger we'd play ping pong. He invariably beat me, which I ascribe to his having an education at the university. It wasn't a case of losing on purpose, either. He was just damn good."

Pulpologist Link Hullar had these remarks about Baumhofer: "His magnificent paintings brought Pete Rice to life, from the first issue through October 1935: twenty-four stirring cover illustrations. The quality of Mr. Baumhofer's work goes far beyond that of the average pulp artist. While there were many capable illustrators and some very talented artists among the ranks of the pulpsters, few were the equal of Walter."

There was a man named Ivan S. Turgeniev who once wrote these words: "A picture may instantly present what a book could set forth only in a hundred pages." Walter Baumhhofer sure proved that beyond all doubt!

Perhaps in closing my remarks about this remarkable artist the reader might like a few personal touches. In a short note to me back in 1980, Walt commented in part: "We live with two cats who don't get along, and who boss us around tremendously. We live in a house built in 1898, except for the two-story-high studio, which is 33 years old. Hope you're interested in this junk."

I've met Walter just once. I've met Saunders just once. but what a joy it was to talk with these men and share if only for a brief time some of their experiences. (We've included a snapshot of Walter, his wife Pete, and artist Franklyn Hamilton in this segment also.)

ROBERT G. HARRIS

The next artist we'd like all of you to meet is Robert G. Harris. His covers were seen on a variety of pulp magazines, including *Wild West Weekly, Western Story Magazine, Pete Rice, Thrilling Western*. This man is by definition "one who professses and practices an art in which conception and execution are governed by imagination and taste." He is a man who enjoys life to its fullest. "I'm mighty proud to have carved a niche alongside some other fine craftsmen," he told me. His laughter rings with merriment. His eyes sparkle with brilliance as he stands in his large studio among the portraits and paintings of both past and present. He is a man who "once into this sacred realm of spirits and turpentine, ground pigment and linen canvas, becomes lost for a short period of time. Lost even to the world."

(We've included a group of covers that Harris selected especially for this book; we hope you enjoy them.)

The reader may wish to check the April 1986 issue of *Echoes* magazine. Its cover has a sketch by Franklyn Hamilton of a Doc Savage cover as painted originally by Harris. There are many readers who associate his art with the portraits of Sonny Tabor and the Oklahoma Kid from *Wild West Weekly*. Author John Dinan said this about Harris: "Western cover artist R. G. Harris, whose style encompasses painstaking realism; perhaps his best cover is on the August 15, 1936 issue of *Wild West Weekly."

Picture this scene if you will: The canvas is empty, resting on an easel. Standing in front of it is Bob Harris, holding a brush. In his mind's eye a picture forms. At first the colors are mere strokes, as he gently manipulates the reds, the blues, the whites, the blacks into a coagulation. Soon a picture emerges—it seems almost like magic!

"There was enough work at the time to keep a very young man busy and very happy, certainly out of mischief," Harris remarked. Those pulp art covers were his career beginning and his main concern at the time was "putting a square meal on the table, and a few bucks left for rent. What happened to this product after it left my hands was of little consequence and not to worry, there were lots more where that came form. It was a terrific training ground for building something artistically meaningful to me in the field of illustration. It took a few years but the rewards were beyond my fondest dreams. I have to acknowledge the pulps for those nice rewards."

As I entered his Arizona studio and gazed uoon the various paintings, a few of which are reproduced with the two of us in this book, those vivid colors leaped right at you. You could feel the life in the figures, smell the drifting gunsmoke as the pistols roared. As Ralph Waldo Emerson once wrote: "The reward of a thing well done is to have done it." I think perhaps Harris would agree with that. Incidentally, there is one particular cover used twice. Those of you who have a copy of *Western Adventures* of October 1940 can compare it to a *Wild West Weekly* issue of May 23,

1936. Harris painted it to illustrate a story called "Powder-Smoke Pardon," an Oklahoma Kid saga by Lee Bond for Wild West Weekly. This a typical picture of the Oklahoma Kid in action. I did a lot of this character," Harris added.

While we're about it, Harris also painted covers for *Doc Savage Magazine*. Pulpologist Will Murray asked me to find out from Harris who was the particular model that he used for Doc Savage. Here is what Harris said: "He was a fine young man I found in New Rochelle, N.Y., where I had my first studio, and where I did my pulp covers. His name was Steve Pender, a good athlete with a fine muscular body. I also used Steve for other modeling assignments. He was an inventive model and could hold a pose. He was kept busy in New Rochelle, for it was a town full of artists. After leaving New Rochelle for Westport, Connecticut, after my pulp years, I lost track of Seve. He was a rare guy. You have to remember that a Doc Savage type would be hard to come by at any time. His looks were mostly dreamed up. Steve Pender didn't look like Doc Savage, but he had the acting ability that brought life to the character."

Not so very long ago we spoke to a former senior editor of Standard Magazines, Jack Schiff. He said: "The pulps were assigned the lower rung of the ladder. Also, characterization wasn't really a prime factor. All writers had a debt to the pulps. It was a training ground." But then he added the comment I used at the very beginning of this segment: "Covers sold the pulps."

121

From the desk of

WALTER M. BAUMHOFER

6/3/82

Dear Wooda:

Thanks for your condolences.

I'm getting along well now,
walking with acane.

I hope you and your wife are
both well

I'm looking forward to
seeing you at next year's
Pulpcon12.

Sincerely,

Walt

122

Wild West Weekly
December 4, 1937
BUD JONES OF TEXAS

To Wooda
all my very best

R G Harris

Robert G Harris

123

4/22/86

Dear Woода —

Looking over some old negatives the other day — ran across one I thought would be of historical interest to you.

This is a picture of me taken in my New Rochelle. N. Y. Studio in 1934. This was a time when I was working a twenty hour day turning out those bloody pulps, the other four hours of my day I spent dreaming about them.

The picture on the easel is the charcoal layin on canvas before painting. It was a job for Thrilling Ranch Stories probably a July 1934 issue. The issue contained stories — "Range Daughter" by George M. Johnson and "Long Rider Law" by Eugene Cunningham.

Painting for cover in upper right hand corner is for Western Round Up magazine. Could be an Aug. 1934 issue. This was a twenty cent magazine, I don't think they were in business long. This issue contained a story by Buck Ringo titled "The great life Story of the missouri badman."

Behind my head on wall hangs some tumble weed I brought back from Taos N. M.

2. Hanging about that is a tommy gun I made of wood as a prop for some adventure type covers. The black oval on other side is a "Tommy Drimes" Stetson (a true 10 gal.) The girl in the oval is wearing this hat. Hanging on the back of my easel is a couple of gun belts and holsters along with a british Pith helmet. The easel is the same easel I use here in my Carefree Studio. A trusty ol' friend — we have been through many a war together.

Hope to see you when you get back from California with your truck load of pulps. My best to Unice ———

See you soon

Bob

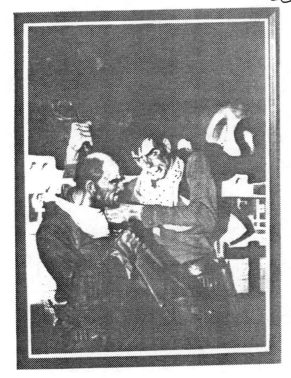

Pete Rice — Western Adventures
November 1935

Thrilling Western
July 1934

To Wooda
from his
friend —

126

C O N C L U S I O N

Growing up in the White Mountain country of Northern Arizona gave me a working knowledge about the working cowboy, along with much respect for him, his land, and even some of those legends surrounding his life. Below is a picture taken during the Forties near Springerville, Arizona. I was in my final year of high school. Most of us wore boots, Levi's, and a wide-brimmed hat. My boots were black with white stars. I also had on a pair of spurs that day.

The corner drug store which was right across from the post office happened to be the place we bought all of our pulp magazines. During those years I spent time at the Diamond Rock Lodge, where one old wrangler taught me most of what I remember about western lore. Diamond Rock was near a place called Buffalo Crossings, location of the CCC camp. We'd also exchange pulp issues of one sort or another, mostly westerns of course. They were kept out in the bunkhouse where eventually most everybody got to read 'em. I suspect that when the issues got all worn out they ended up in the outhouse.

I'd like to finish up by quoting again the words of pulp author FREDERICK C. DAVIS. These words were written to me in a letter some years ago. Incidentally, it was Davis who wrote about a character in *Western Trails* called Duke Buckland. Davis said this about the pulps:

"IT'S A SHAME TO THINK WE'LL NEVER SEE THEIR LIKES AGAIN."

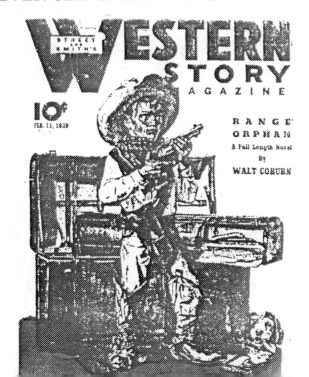

BIBLIOGRAPHY

Dinan, John. *The Pulp Western*. (A Popular History of Western Fiction Magazines in America). San Bernardino, Borgo Press, August, 1983.

Dime Novel Roundup. (A magazine devoted to the collecting, preservation and literature of the old-time dime and nickel novels, libraries and popular story papers.) The following issues were reviewed: December, 1979; February, April, June, August, October, December, 1980; December, 1981.

Goulart, Ron. *Cheap Thrills*, New Rochelle. Arlington House, 1972.

McKinstry, Lohr and Weinberg, Robert. *The Pulp-Hero Index*, Opar Press, June, 1947.

Sampson, Robert. *Yesterday's Faces*, Volume One and Two. Bowling Green University Popular Press, 1983, 1984.

Striker, Fran Jr. *His Typewriter Wore Spurs*.

Jones, Robert Kenneth. *The Shudder Pulps*. West Linn: FAX, 1975.